SHAKEN, RATTLED & ROLLED

A HISTORY OF ROCKABILLY & ROCK 'n' ROLL

'Wildkat' Mike George

First published in Great Britain in 2023

Copyright © Mike George 2023

Published by Victor Publishing - victorpublishing.co.uk

Mike George has asserted his right under the Copyright, Designs and
Patents Act 1988 to be identified as the author of this work.

ISBN: 9798864533796

victorpublishing.co.uk

SHAKEN, RATTLED & ROLLED

A HISTORY OF ROCKABILLY & ROCK 'n' ROLL

'Wildkat' Mike George

CONTENTS

'Wildkat' Mike George

INTRODUCTION

I was just twelve years of age when I first heard of rock 'n' roll. Mum used to play stuff, which upon reflection was quite varied. She liked Muddy Waters, who of course was a blues musician, and Fats Waller, a jazz pianist, Clinton Ford, and a bit later she'd play some Buddy Holly music, which she and I both liked very much. She told me that when the news of his passing was announced in 1959, it seemed like everyone was distraught and in tears. I was intrigued by this...who was this person that generated such an emotional outpouring when he died?

One of the dangers in setting out to write this book, was that many other histories have been written before and I was in danger of copying all the rest. Who would read this? Well there are many people that know the history as well as I do, perhaps in many cases, more so. However, I am a bit of a sceptic, and part of the folklore that is included in many histories are the bullshit and myths surrounding it's beginning, which we were all expected to believe carte blanche. I've always felt that to accept anything at face value is actually of no value at all. And so I began my journey in discovering what had happened, and found a lot of rhetorical rubbish associated with rock 'n' roll. For instance, Colonel Tom Parker's 'publicity machine', more or less re-wrote the history of Elvis' first foray into music. Indeed, Parker was a one man self proclaimed publicity machine! I understood what he was doing, but when one realises that much of what happened before he was even aware of the name, Elvis Presley, then you begin to understand and see through the hype.

Very few of the histories already out there, tell of the gruelling schedule of concerts that Elvis, Scotty (Moore) and Bill (Black) embarked upon, largely on the basis of a few thousand records sold in the local Memphis area. The fact that the reaction to Elvis on this tour, had never been seen before, at least not for a beginner to the business, speaks volumes.

But if you have never heard this music, to any great extent, which is entirely possible, especially if you are one of the millions worldwide that have been force fed by radio stations and the media with such weird and wonderful styles of music as hip hop, garage, rave and whatever the latest craze is. You might be surprised to learn, however much it is denied, that without the advent of rock 'n' roll back in the mid 50's, popular music today would be a very different beast. I also found that there was a whole world of other musical styles, which helped to create rock n' roll, music that was directly linked back to the turn of the century. The plantation songs of the slaves, the 12-bar blues walking bassline and the eight bar boogie woogie piano and some of the lyrics which, when originally performed, in the early 1900's must have sounded new and innovative, but were still being used in the 1950's. This new rockabilly and its descendant, rock 'n' roll, was fresh, exciting, and it was dangerous. But how did it come to be?

Well, I wanted to try and find the answers to these questions, to explore the origins of this music and why it happened. I believe that anything new emerges due to a set of circumstances. For instance, the rise of the National Socialists in Germany came about due to the punitive measures taken by the allies after world war I, the failure of the German economy and the hardships that came with it. This proved fertile ground for any radical form of politics and this allowed Adolf Hitler and his thuggish followers to take advantage of that. So, I asked, what was happening in post war America that opened the door for teenagers and music to change from the relatively safe, big band music of the jazz nee` swing era to the dangerous and exciting new rock 'n' roll music? Rock 'n' roll music was instrumental (no pun intended) in breaking down social and racial barriers in the USA, and that is important. For whilst rock 'n' roll may have been a form of musical entertainment, it also impacted society. Something that had never happened before. I was interested in finding out why a whole generation of youngsters/teenagers rebelled against their parents, the accepted norm and in effect, society. What was it that inspired them to do so?

I also try to explain why, in recent years, various rockabilly and rock 'n' roll revival groups have brought a renewed appreciation for the genre, to the extent that not only is it still popular, but perhaps more so now than it ever was when it first emerged, although it is largely ignored by the mainstream media. At the time, the establishment decided that this new music was a 'craze', that would only last a few months, but, it is still with us.

Rock 'n' roll music in the 1950's was the end, and the beginning. The end, because it relegated jazz, swing (which were much the same thing really) and big band music of the 1940's to being either a specialised or of limited popularity. The beginning, because, although it had evolved from a lot of different influences, it also became a stepping point, a basis from which to evolve into more modern styles of music. These styles have continued to evolve to a point that, thanks in part to new equipment and the development of recording techniques, it can sometimes be very difficult to hear any resemblance to the origins.

Before we go any further, one of the questions that always seems to come up, mainly from people who have never heard the music, is "What is rockabilly and what is the difference between it and rock 'n' roll?" To coin a popular phrase, this is 'opening a can of worms', and quite a large one. But let's give it a go anyway, because you dear reader, need to understand this before we move on.

To return to absolute basics, I will generalise by stating that there were two main sources for rockabilly and later, rock 'n' roll. These were the blues music of the blacks and the Country - hillbilly music of the whites. Rockabilly was the catalyst which evolved into rock 'n' roll, and its major influence was the Hillbilly side of country music, which itself included various different styles. However, rockabilly also included and incorporated blues influences, which then evolved into rock 'n' roll. Just to make it confusing!

As a genre, rockabilly blended the sound of western swing, boogie-woogie, jump blues, country and Hillbilly with that of rhythm and blues, inject an overload of energy and enthusiasm into it and you have rockabilly. The archetypal rockabilly band consisted of upright bass, rhythm and Lead guitar. Later, when keyboards and sax was added, the music changed, leading to what is considered 'classic' rock and roll. The term 'rockabilly' itself is a portmanteau of 'rock' (from 'rock 'n' roll') and 'hillbilly', that contributed strongly to the style. In fact, the word 'rockabilly' was sparsely used, at least not by the musicians, although the word did crop up in some songs and the quite frequently in the media at the time, (notably Billboard and Cashbox) but it certainly wasn't a widely used term in the 1950's to describe the style of music. The word only really came into recognisable use in the 1970's, and is sometimes attributed to Charley Records in the UK, who were actively engaged in releasing rare and long forgotten music from the 1950's. Again, this is 'spin', adopted by Charley records themselves and at the time, not challenged. They weren't however, the only ones using the word. And the contents of the songs, the lyrics, could be about anything; taking a rocket ship to the moon, dancing with a variety of animals, stuttering, large feet..the variety is endless!

Sam Phillips at SUN, the man seen as most responsible for its introduction, hated the term 'Rockabilly', as he saw it as only one stage removed from the derogative 'hillbilly' label. It is useful to briefly explore that use of the word 'hillbilly', as a term derogative or otherwise and why it was hated so much by mainly Southern white musicians. For all of the other influences that went to make up rockabilly, by far the biggest contributing genre was hillbilly music. Indeed, when Elvis was first starting out, he was often a support act to headlining hillbilly acts such as Hank Snow, Ferlin Husky and Faron Young. Pretty soon he was attracting nicknames such as "The Memphis Flash" and "The Hillbilly cat", which he hated, but it's interesting to note that the word cat, short for Hepcat, was actually a term for youngster that would listen to Jump Jive music, such as played by Cab Calloway in the 1940s.

But America had created a stereotype image of hillbillies as corn chewing, dungaree wearing, moonshine distillers that were mostly uneducated, farmworkers from the rural southern states. In actual fact, whilst a few of them worked on farms and in the cotton fields, like many generalisations, it wasn't completely accurate. In fact many songs named as 'hillbilly', were written and created by the writers in big record companies in the north, it's true to say that many of the authors that wrote many of these tunes, had barely stepped out of New York, let alone ventured into the hills of Tennessee!

At it's very beginning, what was classed as 'hillbilly', were actually folk songs, often played with just a guitar and a fiddle, the fiddling, a direct descendant of original British folk music that had come over with the very first immigrants. Record companies, even big ones, didn't send out representatives to record 'in the field', or even search for this type of music, as they were not really aware that there was much interest, other than locally. However, that changed when a fiddle player from Arkansas, Eck Robinson, travelled to New York, ostensibly to ask for a try out, or audition as we would call it today. He recorded two songs, "Arkansas traveller" and "Sally Gooden", for the Victor label, thus becoming the first hillbilly musician ever to be recorded. So popular were these tunes, that recording companies began to think about hunting out hillbilly performers, as well as Jazz and Blues players. This was at a time when the Edison wax cylinders were first being introduced, and they were the first method of listening to music. Then in the 1920's, 'commercial' radio emerged, and hillbilly music was one of it's stars. The recording companies had discovered, and were amazed at the popularity of this early hillbilly music, and that despite a general state of poverty in the south, people still seemed to have the funds to purchase the wax cylinders and listen to the music. And hillbilly music soon threw up it's own stars, Jimmie Rodgers and The Carter Family, being at the forefront. All that notwithstanding, to label someone as a "hillbilly", was seen as derogatory and understandably those on the receiving end, resented it.

From these humble roots, after world war two, hill-billy music, with it's adopted influences and styles such as blues and swing eventually became rockabilly, once of course the teenage musicians had injected a bucket load of pizazz into it!

Rockabilly as we understand it now, was actually only a force as a genre in music for three or four years, during which it burned hotly and brightly, By the middle to late 1950s it had either fused with or been consumed by what we now call rock and roll, to such a degree that it had virtually died out as a distinct musical form, and its performers moved onto other styles and genres.

Another thing that confuses many, are modern bands that claim to be playing rock 'n roll. Certainly they have their roots in rock n' roll, but the noises they make now, wouldn't have been recognised in the 1950's. I have a theory, and it runs along the lines that many bands to this day who play modern evolved forms of rock and heavy metal, for instance, described themselves as playing rock 'n' roll! This I know irritates many of the rock 'n' roll fans, (many of whom live pseudo-50's lifestyles and want nothing whatsoever to do with modern music), to the extent that they began using the word 'rockabilly' to describe any and all rocking music from the 1950's, simply to separate themselves from modern music.

This may or may not have been a deliberate move, but the argument does seem to have some credibility, but in reality it becomes ridiculous to describe such artists as Little Richard as Rockabilly, although just to confuse things a bit more, Chuck Berry did have a rockabilly 'feel' to much of his output!

But all of this is jumping the gun to some extent, because this book is the story of a journey of how music changed and adapted, how it exploded into society's consciousness, how it affected life and ultimately suffered whilst under attack from the establishment, then evolved and somehow managed to survive. So, let's get to it; as Lenny Henry said in his voice over in the Harry Potter films, "(Hold on tight), it's gonna be a bumpy ride!"

'Wildkat' Mike George

'Wildkat' Mike George

CHAPTER ONE

Turn of the Century Origins

The music of African Americans can be traced back to the days of slavery. When transported from Africa, the slaves had no understanding of the language of their captors, and were forbidden to speak their native languages, as captors and slave owners feared they would plan and share escape routes or seek revenge and rebel. Therefore, they sang songs to communicate. These were local folk songs known to themselves. Once on their plantations, their captors would teach them the basics of the English language, simply as a means to communicate and make sure the slaves knew what orders were being given. Believing that these slaves were essentially heathens, they would also preach to them about Christianity, and their musical hymns. The slaves would then sing these songs, which became known as spirituals. Spirituals were a distinctly African American response to American conditions. These earliest form of black musical expression in America merged with African music styles and secular American music forms. Peculiar to these songs were the African rhythms and cadences, with an emphasis on rhythm, and the use of complex poly rhythms still found in African music today. This music told of the struggles and the hard life that the slaves endured, and the spirituals evolved into what we now call the blues, Jazz and gospel music.

In the fields, as slaves were working, you could hear them singing these songs not only to pass the time, but many of the songs incorporated coded messages. Some, like "Follow the Drinking Gourd," "Steal Away," and "Wade in the Water," contained coded instructions for escape. Others, like "(Sometimes I Feel like) A Motherless Child" and "I'm Troubled in Mind," conveyed the feelings of despair that black slaves felt. (The Blues). The spirituals also served as critiques of slavery, using biblical metaphors to protest the enslavement of black people. They expressed the longing of slaves for spiritual and bodily freedom, for safety from harm and evil, and for relief from the hardships of slavery. Some slaves were able to bring musical instruments with them or build new ones in this country. The 'banja' or 'banshaw', now known as the banjo, was one of the African instruments that continued to be built and played in America. Africans in America also fashioned numerous types of drums and percussion instruments from whatever materials they could gather. Slaveholders, however, eventually discovered that African slaves were using drums to communicate among themselves, and by the 1700s drums had been banned on many plantations. Slave fiddlers often provided dance music for the southern white gentry, and the sound we recognize today as country fiddling is partially the product of the slave fiddler.

Most slaves could not afford to purchase them, However, using home-made and makeshift instruments, and their own bodies, they created unique musical ensembles.

In the 1870s, the spirituals began to be recognised as a distinct musical form that revealed the beauty and depth of African American culture, although it is doubtful whether many slave owners thought that way. Beginning in 1871, the Fisk Jubilee Singers toured the United States and Europe performing Negro spirituals for white audiences. Until they brought these songs to national and international attention, Negro spirituals were widely considered crude and embarrassing holdovers from slavery. The success of the Fisk Jubilee Singers spawned a number of similar black jubilee singing groups, and contributed a sense of pride to many newly emancipated blacks.

In the early part of the 1900s, as a result of the work of black composers, the performance of Negro spirituals became a tradition among black singers, particularly singers of classical music. Composers like Harry T. Burleigh, Margaret Bonds and Hall Johnson set the spirituals to piano accompaniment as a means of preserving and perpetuating the beauty of this traditional black music. Ragtime became the first nationally popular form of American music in 1899, when Scott Joplin's "Maple Leaf Rag" enjoyed unprecedented success, selling over a million sheet-music copies. But ragtime was not new in 1899. Documents reveal that it was being played as early as the 1870s. Black musicians spoke of 'ragging a tune' when describing the use of syncopated rhythms, whether in classical compositions, popular songs, or genteel dance tunes. While black musicians could rag tunes on any instrument, the music we call ragtime developed when the piano replaced the violin as the favourite instrument for dance accompaniment. The blues is perhaps the simplest American musical form to explain, and its origins going back to the slave plantations are obvious. And yet it is also the most versatile. Along with jazz, blues takes its shape and style in the process of performance, and for this reason it possesses a high degree of flexibility. Although certain musical and lyrical elements of the blues can be traced back to West Africa, the blues, like the spiritual, is a product of slavery. When and where did the blues originate? No one can say for sure. We know only that it began in the American South during slavery and, in the years following slavery, spread throughout the region as early bluesmen wandered from place to place.

As America moved into the twentieth century, the blues evolved, borrowing elements from such other musical genres as gospel and ragtime. A "country" style, in which a solo singer accompanied himself on an acoustic guitar, also developed. It was played on the farms of share croppers and in honky-tonk gin joints. Early blues was an acoustic musical tradition, and was invented and performed by literally a handful of itinerant musicians in search of day labour. Much has been made of the pared down qualities of the music. Early practitioners, such as Robert Johnson, widely regarded as the father of what we know as 'classical blues' today, relied on the immediacy of a powerful vocal performance with a striking rhythmic counterpoint to captivate his audiences. The music has powerful alliances with African rhythmic and vocal traditions.

The musical structure of the blues is very simple, built upon three main chords. In the standard blues, called the twelve-bar blues, a certain idea is expressed twice in a repeated lyric and then responded to or completed in a third line. As a way of putting his or her own 'signature' on a song, a blues singer will at certain points use vocal scoops, swoops and slurs, imitate sounds of the accompanying instrument (usually a guitar), or add percussive elements to the rendition. The songwriter W.C. Handy popularized the blues when he published his "Memphis Blues" in 1912 and the "St. Louis Blues" in 1914. These two songs created an unprecedented vogue for the blues, and their popularity, and the success of those who sang them, carried the blues all over the world. The 1920s are considered the era of classic blues, a style popularized by black women like Ma Rainey, Bessie Smith, Alb Hunter and Ethel Waters. The soulful sophistication and haunting beauty of their blues performances were altogether new to American audiences. Bessie Smith, perhaps the most famous of the classic blues singers, epitomized the form's emotional power, while Ma Rainey's singing captured its racy, theatrical side.

During the 1920s, interest shifted from classic blues sung by women, to country blues performed most often by men. This 'down-home' blues was sometimes performed with banjo, string or jug band accompaniment, although the favoured instrumental accompaniment was the guitar. In country blues, the vocal quality was gritty, strained and nasal, and the voice was 'played' in a variety of ways. Singers used falsetto techniques, hummed, and achieved percussive effects using both voice and instrument. Among the best-known country blues singers were Charlie Jackson, Blind Lemon Jefferson, Robert Johnson, Blind Boy Fuller (1908-1941), Gus Cannon, and Huddie Ledbetter ("Leadbelly"), who also performed a variety of non-blues folk music.

Post-war America at this time was still segregated, and black culture was the same. Blacks had their own music, their own clubs, their own performers, their own lives. Whites didn't want to mix with the blacks. White Americans had looked down on, abused and ostracised the blacks for years, even in the north, despite the declaration of emancipation and the official abolition of slavery. Certainly, white children would not have had much, if any, contact whatsoever with black society, and certainly wouldn't have been encouraged to do so. It is perhaps quite extraordinary nowadays to think of turning on the radio or watching a TV programme without seeing or hearing a black performer. But that is what life was like in the late 1940's and early 1950's.

Additionally, and perhaps importantly, black musicians were rarely courted by the white-run mainstream record companies, and certainly not afforded the same rights or privileges given to white performers. Often a representative of a record company, many of them independent, might travel hundreds of miles recording a basic acetate of any blues performers, that they came across, 'in the field', visiting villages and townships to record black artists on a portable machine. If the music ever reached the studio, and often it didn't, engineers would produce vinyl records (in 78 rpm format), and distribute them to local radio stations on a black and white basis. The small independent record companies would often have a representative, or perhaps even the owner himself, who would travel sometime hundreds of miles to record local musicians. They would then visit the major record labels in an effort to lease their master recordings to them. This was because the small companies had limited ability to distribute records much further than their local area. If a particular song on record had any commercial appeal, quite often the larger studios would hire a white band, often with professional musicians and perhaps a known star, to record a new version. The original version may have been released, but only after the record company had released and promoted the white version. Those not deemed suitable for white audiences were ignored by the whites.

Only a few compliant black musicians made it in the mainstream. Nat King Cole, for instance, was criticised by the black community because he was seen as a traitor to the black cause, and although performers such as Louis Jordan and Louis Armstrong made successful careers, they were largely patronised by the white run music industry. Further more, many black groups and bands, suffered from prejudice, especially in the Southern states. There were severe segregation rules in place, and black groups often found that they were unwelcome in hotels local to the venue at which they were booked. Some black performers did make it to white venues, but found that they were not permitted to use the venue's facilities, and were often told to go around to the back door, to eat in the kitchens, away from the white patrons. But, essentially, the message from the white run music industry was clear; "we make the rules, play by them or not at all"! Just to ensure that disk jockeys, for instance, were quite clear about the sort of music they had, records performed by black artists often had the words "Race Music" or "Sepia toned" stamped on them. An outrageous concept today, which no doubt the woke, politically correct community would have a blue fit about, but one which the black performers and customers purchasing records welcomed. All of that changed when Jerry Wexler, a Billboard journalist, adopted the term 'rhythm and Blues', in June 1949, and it was suggested that this be adopted as an acceptable label for black blues music. And it was.

The other big powerhouse in music was country and western music, mainly performed, and certainly greatly appreciated, in the rural mid and southern States of America. Going back to the slavery days, the white landowners and slavers saw the slaves with their crude instruments, and began to take them up themselves - especially the fiddle and banjo. Soon they became good enough to perform at local dances, adding a guitar and a bass. Drums occasionally appeared but were rare, a throwback to the banning of drums. Thus began the origins of country music, mixed with rural folk songs, and borrowing rhythms from black performers. However, post war country and western, as it had become known, went into a slump, partly due to having lost many performers to the war. But there were several country and hillbilly performers who had survived and returned, that were influenced by the big band sounds and instrumentation of the jazz-swing orchestras, and incorporated elements into their music. There were crazes as well, such as the boogie woogie piano craze, and these rhythms, created largely by the black music industry, were also borrowed and integrated into country and western by such bands as Bob Wills and his Texas Playboys, Spade Cooley, the Delmore brothers and others. Whilst being an interesting direction to take their music in, it disseminated country and western music, which was suffering.

Despite these doldrums, there were a few bright spots. For instance, Hank Williams emerged as an outrageous talent and galvanised a vulnerable country and western music scene, creating a new sound that today we recognise as Honky Tonk, perhaps because he played a lot of working men's clubs and bars, known as Honky Tonks. Williams would sing about the everyday problems of the ordinary working man, often carrying a heartfelt emotion in his voice that had never been heard before. His problem was that he had a drink and a drug habit. Often, he would miss recording sessions and even concert dates, because he was either drunk or under the influence of one drug or another. He passed away in 1953, in the back of a car that was taking him to a concert.

Hank Williams

America had emerged from the war with a renewed self-confidence, more or less financially intact, and full of hope with grand new ideas. However, the first faint rumblings in the world of musical entertainment would herald dramatic changes, which the establishment, at least, could never have envisaged.

CHAPTER TWO

Party Time

After World War II, the United States was in better economic condition than any other country in the world. Even the 300,000 combat deaths suffered by Americans paled in comparison to any other nations involved in the war.

Building on the economic base left after the war, American society became more affluent in the post-war years than most Americans could have imagined in their wildest dreams, before or during the war. Public policy provided money for veterans to attend college, to purchase homes, and to buy farms.

The overall impact of such policies was almost incalculable, but it certainly aided returning veterans to better themselves and to begin forming families and having children in unprecedented numbers. But not all Americans participated equally in these expanding life opportunities, and in the growing economic prosperity.

The image and reality of overall economic prosperity and the upward mobility it provided for many white Americans was not lost on those blacks and poor whites, who had largely been excluded from the full meaning of the American Dream, both before and after the war.

The reality for many, was that countless veterans came back to America, and many of them had a difficult time readjusting to civilian life. They searched for the adventure and adrenaline rush associated with life at war, that had now left them. Civilian life felt too monotonous for many, and they craved the danger which they had become accustomed to. Others sought the close bonds and camaraderie they had found in the forces. One of the main ways they came together was in Motorcycling. Although a popular pre-war pursuit, motorcycling emerged stronger than ever as a substitute for wartime experiences. Men who had been a part of the motorcycling world before the war were now joined by thousands of new members.

The hiatus of this obsession with motorcycles came on July 3, 1947, when an annual fourth of July gypsy tour event began in Hollister, California. Hollister was a very small hick town, with a population of just over 2,500 (it only has a population of 20,000 today). Around 4,000 motorcyclists turned up, many of them in self-styled clubs called, variously, the 13 Rebels, Pissed Off Bastards of Bloomington, the Boozefighters, the Market Street Commandos, the Top Hatters Motorcycle Club, and the Galloping Goose Motorcycle Club. This influx almost doubled the population of the small town. They came from all over the United States, and Hollister was completely unprepared for the number of people that arrived. Initially the motorcyclists were welcomed into the Hollister bars, as the influx of people meant a boom in business. But soon, drunken bikers were drag racing their bikes through the small streets of Hollister and consuming huge amounts of alcohol, from which fighting broke out and there was some vandalism. Things got out of hand and the small, seven-man police force of Hollister was overwhelmed by the influx, and soon lost control.

The press heard about the disturbances and blew the whole thing dramatically out of all proportion, describing it as an 'invasion', and 'pandemonium', exaggerating the damage and violence, with headlines describing such as; "HAVOC IN HOLLISTER! – Motorcyclists take over town – Many Injured".

The event was also largely responsible for the later formation of the Hells Angels and other motorcycle gangs. More importantly, it was the first indication of the difficulty returning servicemen found when trying to adjust to civilian life. Many of them found that they couldn't find work, the jobs they had held prior to the war, and were promised would be safe, were not. Those that didn't ride motorcycles also experienced difficulties with their relationships, with wives whom some of them hadn't seen in three or four years, and the divorce rate rose.

However, whilst a proportion of returning servicemen did find problems adjusting to life, just as many did not, and within a very short time, there was a baby boom. These baby boomers would become significant in a few years. It seemed everyone was looking for something to latch on to, and of course, many turned to music.

After World War II, the big band sounds of many wartime orchestras, such as Benny Goodman, Tommy Dorsey and even Glenn Miller, began to lose their mainstream popularity, gradually being replaced by an army of young crooners and vocal pop performers, such as the orchestra backed Frank Sinatra, Dean Martin, Perry Como, and Andy Williams. It was tuneful, it was bright and gay, but it was without doubt, safe and bland, much of it performing the same, harmless melodies, guaranteed not to upset anyone. There were the occasional oddities, such as the deaf Johnny Ray, who cried his way through his ballads with tears of emotion, often tearing at his hair, falling to the floor, still singing. Ray quickly earned the nicknames "Mr. Emotion", "The Nabob of Sob", "The Prince of Wails" and several others. Young girls queued for hours to see him, and screamed in much the same way that they did for young Frank Sinatra. Children on the whole though, were expected to follow their parent's example, dress like them, or at least how their parents wanted them to dress, and listen to (and appreciate) what they did. They secretly didn't, but weren't brave enough to buck any particular trend at that time. Things would soon change.

The post-war world presented America, and indeed the rest of the world, with a number of problems and issues. Flushed with their success against Germany and Japan in 1945, most Americans initially viewed their place in the post-war world with optimism and confidence. This was in contrast to Great Britain, who had seen their top spot in the world, their commonwealth, all but eroded. Britain was suffering with huge debt, mostly from the cost of the war and the land-lease programme, a policy under which the United States supplied Great Britain, the Soviet Union and other Allied nations with food, oil, and materiel between 1941 and 1945. The cost of the lend-lease programme has been estimated at $11.3 billion, or $180 billion in today's currency. Of course, not all of it was Britain's debt, but a sizable chunk was. Great Britain's 'party' would happen later and would involve a musical invasion of the USA and would herald a decade, now known as the 'swinging sixties'. But, until then, it was a case of austerity and rationing all the way, and this would last until the mid-1950's. Having said that, it would be wrong to suggest that Great Britain was not partying to some extent, and whilst the 60's in Britain was known, mainly by the media, as a period of "free love", this is actually incorrect. In fact, this concept had its origins in the 1950's, but only reached its zenith in 1964, when the pill was made available for the first time. The seeds of this came from the 50's. But I digress.

Within two years of the end of the war, new challenges and perceived threats had arisen to erode American confidence - at least their confidence on the world stage. There were new tensions and small wars. By 1948 a new form of problem had emerged. The Cold War was a rise in relationships between the United States, the Soviet Union, and their allies. In the next 20 years, the Cold War spawned many tensions between the two superpowers abroad, and fears of Communist subversion, exemplified by McCarthyism, an anti communist programme, inspired by Senator Joseph McCarthy that gripped domestic politics in America. One of the stranger by products of the cold war, was the space race, which effectively was a power struggle between the U.S.A. and Soviet Union.

The Soviets were the first to put a man into orbit, and it heralded a declaration by President Kennedy, that America would put a man on the moon, which they did in the late 1960's, thus giving America the right to say they had won! The US, Britain and its allies were also involved in tensions in Korea, the Middle East and Cuba, all as a result of, and indeed part of, the Cold War.

In fact, America's economy was very much intact, and indeed buoyant, (as opposed to Britain who were very much, by comparison, the poor, destitute partners). Even though some economists had predicted a new crisis of mass unemployment and inflation, history proved the pessimists wrong. U.S. factories that had proven so essential to the war effort, quickly mobilized for peacetime, rising to meet the needs of consumers, who had been encouraged to save up their money in preparation for just such a post-war boom.

American consumers were eager to spend their money on everything from big-ticket items like homes, cars and furniture, to appliances, clothing, shoes and everything else in between. U.S. factories answered the call, beginning with the auto mobile industry. Car manufacturers encouraged their designers to use their imaginations, seemingly regardless of cost. Given such a free hand, they made hay, designing wonderful, fantastic and fanciful cars that were dripping in mod cons and innovative new ideas, often influenced by science fiction and the space race.

By the mid 1950's nearly every car dripped with bright colours, chrome and sported a set of fins. It worked. New car sales quadrupled between 1945 and 1955, and by the end of the 1950s some 75 percent of American households owned at least one car.

In other areas the trend continued. There was a huge wave of home building, with experimental new developments made famous by William J. Levitt and his company, Levitt & Sons. The communities offered attractive alternatives to cramped central city locations and apartments.

The Veterans Administration and the Federal Housing Administration (FHA) guaranteed that qualified veterans could buy housing for a fraction of rental costs. The first Levittown home sold for $7,900, and in a short period of time 17,000 units were sold, providing homes for 84,000 people.

In addition to normal family dwellings, Levittowns provided private meeting areas, swimming pools, public parks, and recreational facilities. Production was modelled on assembly lines in 27 steps, with construction workers each trained to perform one step. A house could be built in one day with 36 men. Sales in the original Levittown began in March 1947. 1,400 homes were purchased during the first three hours.

Levittown

Music, in contrast to the economy, had become a little staid in the mainstream; indeed, popular music was at a crossroads, and no one was sure where it was going. Post-war radio, which we now consider to be one of the major sources of popular music, in various formats, had only developed into something like we know it today after the war, but even then, was a vastly different medium to what it has since become. The first commercial radio stations began in the 1920's, but they were almost all broadcasting live orchestras. Any speech that was broadcast was by faceless and anonymous continuity announcers who never gave out their names, and followed strict guidelines and language. Although these faceless voices were the fore runners of the disk jockey they, and the radio stations that employed them, had little or no awareness of the influence and power that was theirs to use in peacetime and, radio stations bosses were appalled at the thought of their employees becoming 'personalities'.

It was only in 1906 that the first radio transmission was broadcast, and that was by Reginald A. Fessenden, an electrical Engineer best known for his pioneering work developing radio technology, including the foundations of amplitude modulation (AM) radio. Fessenden made this claim to the first radio broadcast in 1932, but there was little evidence for it because no one was able to listen to the broadcast! This claim was disputed some years later by Lee De Forest, who claimed to have been the pioneer, his first broadcast supposedly made in 1907. However, De Forest became known as 'The Father of Radio', and he wrote a book of the same title that was published in 1950.

The main reason radio broadcasting companies didn't like the idea of recorded music being played, was the inferior quality of the phonographic records. In fact, so passionate was their opposition, they attempted to have the practice banned! But radio was saved by the many independent radio broadcasters who DID play music over the air, mainly because they couldn't afford to book and record live orchestras, nor did they have the premises to do so! With recorded music came the need for announcers, and with the announcers came the personalities. And, with the personalities came, almost hand in hand, the characters, the unhinged, the wild and the downright crazy! Often phonographic 78 rpm records, made of brittle shellac, would be smashed live on air if the disk jockey didn't like the particular piece of music. By the late 1940's radio broadcasting was in full swing, with Disk Jockeys and their personalities ruling the airwaves. Radio stations would be closely associated with the recording companies, the latter hoping to get the former to 'push' their latest releases, and the latest musical crazes. And there were crazes...Western Swing, Hillbilly and, of course, boogie woogie. None of these styles were sustainable in their purest form, and were often incorporated and mixed into other musical styles, most notably into Country and black music.

Black music was immensely popular in America before World War II, especially in the south, where most of America's blacks lived in the rural areas, with only a few isolated pockets living in the north and north east. These northern blacks were the remnants of the comparatively few blacks that escaped the southern slave states at the end of the American Civil War. Although this exodus had slowed, the majority of the blacks still lived in the south. Thus, for the radio executives of the major labels, there was no particular reason to aim programmes at the blacks, or indeed play black music. Conversely, it was the south that pioneered programmes aimed at the black population. Certainly, pre-war, there were numerous stations in the south presenting radio programming that included live and recorded performances of blues, rhythm and blues, and gospel.

With the advent of World War II, there began a surge in migration of blacks, who of course were called up to the north to complete their training, and later serve their country. With this military mobilization came a civilian migration, as their families followed and most of the work was in the north. But whilst this was significant, it didn't much improve the lives of the blacks within society. Yes, the blacks had, like their white counterparts, been shipped off to Europe and other places to fight the war on America's behalf. Yes, they had died alongside their white comrades in arms. But, in fact, they found that, rather than being valued for their service upon their return, the black soldiers were still treated like second class citizens. They were still subject to the Jim Crow laws, much as they had been before the war.

The Jim Crow laws were a collection of state and local statutes that legalized racial segregation. Named after a black minstrel show character, the laws, which existed for about 100 years, from the post-Civil War era until 1968, were meant to marginalize African Americans by denying them the right to vote, hold jobs, receive an education, or take advantage of any other opportunities. Those who attempted to defy the Jim Crow laws often faced arrest, fines, jail sentences, violence and/ or death. The roots of these Jim Crow laws began as early as 1865, immediately following the ratification of the 13th Amendment, which abolished slavery in the United States. The codes, aimed only at the blacks, were strict local and state laws that detailed when, where and how formerly enslaved people could work, and for how much compensation. The codes appeared throughout the south as a legal way to put black citizens into indentured servitude, to take voting rights away, to control where they lived and how they travelled, and to seize children for labour purposes. The legal system was stacked against black citizens, with former Confederate soldiers working in the police judicery, making it difficult for them to win court cases and ensuring they were subject to the codes. These codes worked in conjunction with labour camps for the incarcerated where blacks, free or otherwise, were treated as enslaved people.

Black offenders typically received longer sentences than their white equals, and because of the gruelling work conditions and the way they were treated, often did not survive their sentences. Once released, if they survived, rather than return to the rural south, the blacks stayed in the north and stuck with their own kind.

But, whilst in theory blacks had been set free from slavery by the 13th Amendment, they found that the north was not immune to the Jim Crow type laws either. Some states required black people to own property before they could vote. Schools and neighbourhoods were segregated, and businesses displayed "Whites Only" signs. Returning black veterans met with segregation and violence.

So, of course, they tended to congregate and live in their own areas, creating what became known as ghettos. With them, they bought their culture and, of course, their music. This population shift heralded a change in attitude from the major radio stations in places such as Detroit and Chicago, who realised that suddenly they DID have a sizeable population of blacks to cater for, and they began to play Jazz and blues in an effort to appeal to black listeners. This in turn would lead to a growing interest and popularity of the music, hitherto unheard of by whites or northern born blacks, at least not on a regular basis.

The phrase "rocking and rolling" originally described the movement of a ship on the ocean, but it was also used extensively by the blacks in their patois and language to describe the sexual act. Various gospel, blues and swing recordings used the phrase before it became used more frequently, but still intermittently, in the late 1930s and 1940s, principally on recordings and in reviews of what became known as "rhythm and blues" music aimed solely at black audiences. In 1939, during the April 5th broadcast on "The Fred Allen Town Hall Tonight Show" the song "Rock and Roll" appeared as a barber shop quartet lead-in.

In May 1942, long before the concept of rock and roll had been defined, a Billboard record review described Sister Rosetta Tharpe's vocals on the upbeat blues song "Rock Me", by Lucky Millinder, as "rock-and-roll spiritual singing". But the first reference to "rock n' roll" that most historians can find and agree on, featured the two words in secular content in 1922, when blues singer Trixie Smith recorded "My Man Rocks Me (with One Steady Roll)".

Sister Rosetta Tharpe

Of course, it wasn't just black music that was popular, but the country and western music of the rural south was everywhere south of the Mason-Dixon line - a reference to a demarcation line along the southern Pennsylvania border later to became known, informally, as the boundary between the Southern slave states and Northern free states. Here there was a wealth of styles and music, varied in style and influence. There was honky tonk and hillbilly, although the word was sometimes used as a derogatory term, and western swing, a form of country-based music that contained swing and jazz influences; and in and around Louisiana there was Cajun music, a style sung in Cajun French, often using accordions, and in itself related to Arcadian folk music. And, of course, there was gospel, which was hugely influential, mainly because the southern states were especially full of people with an almost fanatical religious fervor. In addition there were musical crazes, which mostly died out after a short while, but one craze endured and that was boogie woogie. It became a basis for almost all rockabilly and rock n' roll which followed later. Invented by a black piano player called, Clarence "Pine top" Smith, who in 1928, recorded "Pine top's boogie woogie" for the Vocalion label. Boogie woogie was an 8 bar, bass heavy style of percussive piano playing, and although it had been evolving for a while, it was Smith who bought it into the mainstream. It defined the form of the music to perfection and proved to be a game changer. Strangely enough, shortly after recording it Smith passed away and would never see the impact of what he'd created.

There had always been musicians who had a 'sound' before then. When I say they had a sound, they did, but were unable to say what it was. It definitely wasn't jazz, and it was too upbeat to be called country and western. It often sounded like hillbilly, it sometimes had elements of rhythm and blues in it.It was very energetic and, to our sophisticated ears today, would probably be identified as country or, if you're particularly well attuned, hillbilly. Most of the performers were youngsters who borrowed guitar techniques from either country pickers (also known as 'chicken pickers') such as Joe Maphis, or from Jazz guitarists, such as Belgian, Django Rheinhardt, who often played intricate and complicated guitar breaks. The worst thing, for them at least, was that no one in the music industry was interested. Most of the time these musicians would get together in a garage or perhaps a local hall, perhaps even at a local dance, but they were unable to break through into the mainstream. They weren't really aware of what they were doing, other than having fun. It is conceivable that they probably didn't even have any ambition to record or become 'stars'. But first, there was a subtle change of attitudes and perceptions of life, that the youngsters were beginning to go through, that played an important part in what they were doing. In 1953, Marlon Brando, at the time a young and upcoming actor, starred in the film, "The Wild One". The film was loosely based on the events at Hollister, with a motorcycle gang taking over a town. It was Brando's performance that caught the eye, and propelled his career. During the film, he was asked: "What are you rebelling against, Johnny"? Brando, without batting an eyelid, drawled back lazily, "What have you got"?

Then in 1955, came the film, "Rebel without a cause", starring James Dean. Again the performance of Dean and the attitudes that were displayed were the talking points. These performances displayed a degree of rebelliousness that America society found difficult to deal with. But, they did display an attitude that was beginning to emerge with American youth. Suddenly it was OK to NOT blindly follow what your parents taught, to wear what they wore or to listen to the music that they listened to. The stage was then set for a huge change and that included in music.

It was in 1954 that an event came along that changed everything and effectively opened the door for all those musicians that had a sound and for even more that didn't. And it was almost by accident. That the music changed was down to a combination of the vision of a record label and studio owner, Sam Phillips, who became aware of a truck driver, a 19-year-old Elvis Aaron Presley, and a moment of tomfoolery which stumbled upon a sound that was to define the music and open the door for hundreds, perhaps thousands, of others and, ultimately, change the course of popular music forever.

CHAPTER THREE
Sun Rise

In the 1940s, Sam Phillips had worked as a DJ and radio engineer for station WLAY in Muscle Shoals, Alabama. According to Phillips, the station's 'open format' (of broadcasting music by white and black musicians alike) would later inspire his work in Memphis. Beginning in 1945 he worked for four years as an announcer and sound engineer for radio station WREC in Memphis.

On January 3, 1950, Phillips opened The Memphis Recording Service at 706 Union Avenue in Memphis. He had a sign on the front window stating that anyone could record there and, for a fee, would be presented with an acetate disc of their recording. He also recorded wedding and birthday parties. On the professional side, The Memphis Recording Service also served as the studio for Phillips's own label, Sun Record Company, which he launched in 1952. Phillips encouraged musicians to come and record at the studio.

He recorded different styles of music, but was interested in the blues: "The blues, it got people... black and white... to think about life, how difficult, yet also how good it can be. They would sing about it, they would pray about it, they would preach about it. This is how they relieved the burden of what existed day in and day out."

In a short while Sun gained the reputation throughout Memphis as a label that treated local artists with respect and honesty, regardless of status. Phillips provided a non-critical, spontaneous environment that invited creativity and vision.

He was patient and willing to listen to almost anyone who came in off the street to record. Memphis was a happy home to a diverse musical scene: gospel, blues, hillbilly, country, boogie, and western swing. Taking advantage of this range of talent, there were no style limitations at the label. Phillips recorded what the music historian Peter Guralnick considered the first rock and roll record: "Rocket 88", by Jackie Brenston and His Delta Cats, at least that was what Sam Phillips had written on the label.

In fact they were a band led by then 19-year-old Ike Turner, who also wrote the song, called The Kings of Rhythm. Why they recorded at SUN without insisting that this was the name of the group is lost in the mists of time. The recording was made in Memphis and was leased to Chess Records in Chicago, who duly released it in 1951. Phillips could see there were changes that were happening in music, but was frustrated that he was unable to quite understand what they were. Famously, he was quoted as saying if he could find a white singer that could sing like a Negro, then he would make a million dollars. What happened next was a series of coincidences that question those who state there is no such thing as fate.

Sam Phillips

So, there was a strange student attending Humes High School in Memphis. His name was Elvis Aaron Presley. He was by any measure unusual, but compared to his fellow students he was downright weird. He was shy, and had a very close, and some might say oddly disturbing, relationship with his mother, who doted on him. He would often be found hanging around on Beale Street in Memphis, listening to the black performers singing the blues in all its forms. He not only listened to the music; he absorbed it. But it wasn't just the blues - he would listen to almost anything, from the likes of Sister Rosetta Tharpe, through the Arcadian (Cajun) music of Louisiana, to the crooning of Frank Sinatra and Dan Martin. He took it all in. He learned to played a few chords on the guitar, but also absorbed the sights and sounds. He noted the colourful way that the blacks dressed, wearing black and white saddle shoes, wide shantung silk peg trousers and loud shirts, complemented by a variety of equally loud jackets. Elvis grew his hair long and kept it greased, with long sideburns, aping the truck drivers he saw in his place of work as a lorry driver at The Crown Electric Company. As for aping the black's style of dress, he sported the same.

His favourite colours were rose pink and black, and he would often gaze through the windows at Lansky's, a Memphis clothing store that almost exclusively sold fashions to the black community. The story goes, he was invited in one day and asked what he was doing, to which he replied that he was a singer and that one day, once he became famous, he would come into the store and kit himself out with some of the Lansky Brothers' stock. Reportedly, he was given an account and told to take what he needed. It is, without doubt, the sort of exaggerated story that would be peddled by Colonel Tom Parker a few years later. It is more than likely untrue, as it's almost inconceivable that anyone would run their business in that way. However true the story is, it is important, since Elvis' 'image', whether contrived or not, would set the guidelines for future performers to ensure that, at least on stage, they would flaunt flamboyant attire.

Elvis wanted to be a singer, a performer, and he was single mindedly hunting around for opportunities. He auditioned for an amateur gospel quartet called The Songfellows, as one of the group was leaving and they were seeking a replacement.

However, following Presley's audition, the original group member decided to stay.

In May 1953 he auditioned at the Hi-Hat in Memphis as a vocalist for a band, but Eddie Bond, the owner of the Hi-Hat, turned him down. Colonel Tom Parker claimed this was a case of short sightedness by Bond. Parker was creating a myth and putting together a biographic, romanticised picture of Elvis that often ventured into wild exaggeration, to try and create an aura around Elvis. The most famous one was that, according to later stories, released after he had signed for RCA, Elvis visited Sun Studio on July 18, 1953, with the idea of cutting a disk under their recording service deal as a present for his mother. He paid $3.98 to record the first of two double-sided demo acetates, "My Happiness" and "That's When Your Heartaches Begin". In fact, this is almost certainly untrue, as the Presley household did not own a record player at the time! But that was a minor fact, to be duly ignored!

The story is typical of Parker's ability to create an aura around Elvis. Parker would, however, never let a fact get in the way of his narrative. Don't forget that Parker was not around when Elvis first visited the Sun Studio, and would not even have been aware he existed! Although Elvis did reportedly give the acetate to his mother as a much-belated extra birthday present some time later. (Incidentally, that one-off acetate has since been valued at $500,000 by Record Collector magazine). What is nearer to the truth is that Elvis was ambitious and visited Sun with only one purpose

- to impress Sam Phillips, with a view to being taken on.

Anyway, according to the story, he was 'noticed' by the Sun Studio secretary, Marion Keiser, who made a note of his name and later brought him up in conversation with Sam Phillips, who had been away at the time. Asked by Marion Kaiser who he sounded like, the story goes, Elvis replied "I don't sound like anybody".

On January 4, 1954, he returned to Sun Studios to record a second acetate, "I'll Never Stand in Your Way" / "It Wouldn't Be the Same Without You". He did, of course, come to the notice of Sam Phillips, but that was entirely thanks to Marion Kaiser, as she and Phillips were not only close, but in fact were involved in an on-off affair. It is very difficult these days to listen to those early recordings and understand why Sam Phillips was intrigued to find out more. To our modern ears he had a high voice, almost a falsetto, and was in tune, but very little suggests that he sounded anything more than a kid who had come in off the street to make a recording. Phillips had acquired a demo recording of "Without You", but was unable to identify the vocalist, when Marion reminded him about the young truck driver. She called him on May 26, 1954, and again we return to Colonel Tom Parker's storytelling.

Parker later claimed that Elvis was so keen that he had run all the way, and arrived at the studio before Marion had even managed to put the phone back into the cradle! This conveniently ignores the fact that the young Elvis was living at Lauderdale Courts, nearly three miles away and would have broken the world land speed record to have achieved it! In any case, Presley was not able to do justice to the song (the original acetate of the song Phillips presented to Elvis, resides in the Memphis State University collection). But Phillips asked him to perform some of the many other songs he knew. After running through a few songs, Presley expressed an interest in finding a band to play with, and Phillips was curious enough to contact two local musicians, Bill Black, a bass Player and Scotty Moore, a guitarist, who, when not playing with Doug Pointdexter and his Starlight Wranglers, would sometimes do some session work for Phillips. He asked them to go and check out this kid and report back to him. They did so on Sunday, July 4, 1954, at Moore's house. Moore reported back to Sam Phillips that neither he nor Bill Black were overly impressed, but they agreed that an exploratory studio session might be useful to see if he had any potential. Again, this sounds a bit odd. If Moore and Black were not that impressed, why would they recommend using valuable studio time to hear more of him?

On July 5, 1954, the trio met at Sun studios to rehearse and record a handful of songs. According to Moore, the first song they recorded was "I Love You Because", but that hadn't worked. They asked Presley what he knew, and discovered that his repertoire was enormous. He had listened to and absorbed a breath-taking array of different music, ranging from crooners to down home blues and almost everything in between! After an exhausting session that wasn't going anywhere, around a quarter to one in the morning on a hot summer night, they decided to take a break. During this break Presley began messing about with Arthur Crudup's "That's All Right (Mama)", essentially, a blues song.

When the other two musicians joined in, Phillips popped his head out of the small engineering booth and asked what they were doing... he got them to restart and began taping. This was the bright, upbeat sound he had been looking for. After the recording was done, they listened to the playback, and Bill Black, known for his acerbic wit, remarked, "Damn. Get that on the radio and they'll run us out of town."

Once again, this sounds like a typical piece of Parker spin that made a rather mundane event sound better than it was. However, as everyone seems to say more or less the same when re-telling the story, and with a lack of any alternative, let's just be gracious and accept this version. Having got one track down, Sam and the band tried loads of other songs to go with it, before they later recorded an up-tempo version of Bill Monroe's "Blue Moon of Kentucky" for the B-side.

The song was originally recorded by Bill Monroe in 2/2 time, a ponderously slow rendition, so they speeded it up to 4/4 time and recorded it. Incidentally, when Monroe later heard Elvis' up-tempo version of his song, he hated it, but strangely he returned to the studio himself and copied it!

Phillips knew he had something different, so to gauge professional and public reaction, Phillips took several acetates of the session to DJ Dewey Phillips (no relation) of Memphis radio station WHBQ's Red, Hot and Blue show.

Dewey Phillips' on-air persona was a speed-crazed hillbilly, with a frantic delivery and entertaining sense of humour. He also had a keen ear for music the listening public would enjoy, and he aired both black and white music, which was abundant in post-World War II Memphis. Memphis was a booming river city which attracted large numbers of rural blacks and whites, along with their individual musical traditions. So, he gave the record its first play on July 8, 1954.

The response was explosive. No one had heard anything like it. Apparently, Elvis was so worried about the response the record would receive, that he went to a local cinema, and it was only when the radio station began receiving phone calls jamming their switchboard, that he was found and dragged into the studio to be interviewed by Dewey Phillips.

His first question was telling. He asked Elvis where he had been to school, and when he answered that it was Humes High, everyone knew that Elvis was white. Dewey Phillips later confirmed this story as true.

A week later Sun had received some 6,000 advanced orders for "That's All Right" / "Blue Moon of Kentucky," which was released on July 19, 1954. From August 18 through December 8, "Blue Moon of Kentucky" was consistently higher on the charts, and then both sides began to chart across the South. The general consensus amongst music historians is that Sam Phillips, and the performance of Elvis Presley in the studio that night, July 5, 1954, changed the sound, feel and style of popular music forever.

CHAPTER FOUR

Rockabilly Explodes

Elvis Presley was not the be all and end all of rockabilly music, nor was he the greatest musician. But the influence and impact of his first foray into recorded music is such that the reader should understand that without Elvis doing what he did at Sun, rockabilly might never have emerged at all.

So, whilst record sales for all of Elvis' Sun releases were good, comparatively for Sun Records, they didn't sell enough to break into the national charts, but they created an effect, and it was an effect that got noticed throughout the American music industry. Sam Phillips recorded and released six records over the next 18 months by Elvis, Scotty and Bill (as they were known), and the trio were sent out on a huge tour of the southern states under the guidance of Bob Neal, a local DJ. playing clubs and halls across the Southern states, sometimes as a support act, sometimes as the headliner. Looking back on the tour dates, it was a crucifying schedule with barely a day off, and often required some 200-300 miles travelling every day between dates. Phillips had realised that Elvis needed a manager and had duly appointed Bob Neal to look after him. One of the dates Elvis played was on 2nd October, 1954, at the legendary 'Grand Ole Oprey' in Nashville. He'd already been approached by the rival 'Louisiana Hayride', but decided to play the Oprey first, to see if he could make it. As it turned out, Elvis bombed, unappreciated by a traditional country audience, and the owner, Jim Denny, famously whispered to him that he should "stick to driving a truck as he'd never make a singer". Elvis vowed never to play the Oprey again (he didn't) and almost immediately signed up with the Hayride as a resident performer, making his debut on 16th October 1954. Elvis would appear, in between other tour dates, and the legend began.

The tour dates took him right across the Southern states of America, and it is significant because amongst those watching in the audiences at various places, were many of those young musicians who had a sound, but didn't know how to exploit it. Buddy Holly, was one of them, and having seen Elvis, immediately changed his act. For some reason, Elvis would shake his leg and wiggle about to the beat of the music, and it was noticed that many of the young ladies became excited with this overt display of suggested sexuality from this outrageously good looking young man. The more they shrieked, the more Elvis did it. Quite often, boyfriends became jealous and would wait for Elvis in the parking lots, and there were many instances of Elvis needing a police presence to allow him to leave the building. In more than a few instances there were reports of gangs of young men and Elvis fighting.

Hovering in the wings was one Colonel Parker. Tom Parker (born Andreas Cornelis van Kuijk) a Dutch-born musical entrepreneur and former 'carnie', a fairground worker that toured with travelling carnivals. Parker arrived illegally in the United States at the age of 20, changed his name, and claimed to have been born in the United States. His Dutch birthplace and immigrant status were not revealed for many years. (It was later rumoured that he was wanted in connection to a murder in Holland, but this was never investigated or proved).

He had, at some point, assisted Jimmie Davis's campaign to become Governor of Louisiana. Once elected, Davis, as a reward, gave him the honorary rank of "Colonel" in the Louisiana State Militia. Parker moved into music promotion in 1938, working with one of the first popular crooners, Gene Austin, and then country music singers Eddy Arnold and Hank Snow. It appeared that very few people who met Tom Parker liked him as a person, considering him brash and boorish, but almost to a man they agreed that he knew how to sell a product.

This was because of his history and background, where he often had to survive on wits and intuition. So the story goes, he once got hold of some sparrows, painted them yellow and then placed them on a hot plate where they would jump about...he sold them as dancing canaries! This was a man that would attempt to sell ice to the Eskimos, and probably succeed! He was about to discover the biggest meal ticket of the rest of his life.

Colonel Tom Parker, still the manager of Hank Snow, had by now heard of this exciting new performer and, never one to bypass a potential to make money, went to see him at one of his appearances. Impressed, he immediately booked him to appear on the undercard of one of Hank Snow's concerts. Snow watched from the wings and was horrified by the reaction that Elvis got. There was no way that he could compete with this! Within a very short time Colonel Parker ended his management of Hank Snow and, unbeknown to Sam Phillips, convinced Bob Neal to appoint

Tom Parker and 'his boy'

him as an advisor, allowing him to promote Elvis. Not long afterwards he would take over as Elvis' Manager. Whilst Bob was happy to help out, he knew that he couldn't promote Elvis in the same way as the fast talking, entrepreneurial Tom Parker could. It enraged Phillips that Parker had gone behind his back. Although he had met Tom Parker, he didn't trust him and certainly didn't like him. He had recognised Bob as a steady, conventional guy who would nurture the young Elvis in a sensible, but conservative, manner, and had chosen him carefully. Phillips saw Tom Parker as a flashy, unconventional and vulgar man that would not have Elvis' best interests at heart. In contrast, Parker quickly realised that as long as Elvis was signed to Sun records, his appeal would be nothing more than local.

Parker, for all his faults, recognised that Elvis was different and that, at least for a while, he would rattle the cage of the music industry. Within a short time, therefore, a rumour had started, presumably by Parker, that Elvis' contract was up for sale. Sam Phillips was initially furious, but began to think about what he could do with the proceeds from the sale of Elvis' contract. At the time he ran SUN records almost as a one-man band. Although there were others who helped out with marketing and distribution, it was Phillips who had the final say on recording, and what was released. Whilst he had recordings in the can, he was unable to release them because, not to put too fine a point on it, SUN was almost broke, with less than $500 in the bank. So, when various record company agents began contacting him and big record companies beginning to circle like vultures over his ailing SUN, he was at a point where, if someone came up with a decent offer, then he felt duty bound to consider it. Mitch Miller, head of Colombia, made an enquiry and was told by Parker that the price would be $25,000. Miller was astonished and flatly refused to discuss the prospect further. Parker also approached Decca and several other companies, but none would go anywhere near the Colonel's valuation. Then, one day, Phillips returned to his office and was confronted by Parker and three executives from RCA with an offer for Elvis' contract. The price was $40,000, $5,000 of which was for the back catalogue and add-ons. This was a huge amount at the time for a relatively unknown artist. The sale was important as it would open a myriad of opportunities, not just for Elvis, but also for Phillips, who saw an opportunity to pay off his mounting debts and bring on some new artists. Phillips, after some negotiating, finally agreed.

The sale of Elvis' contract to RCA, caused a tidal wave of reaction throughout the music industry. $40,000 at that time was, on the face of it, an outrageous and unprecedented sum for any artist, let alone one relatively unknown outside of Memphis and the surrounding area. Even Frank Sinatra, who was the world's top entertainer at the time, didn't have a contract worth that much! To put that into perspective, today that sum is the equivalent of about $450,000! Although it was big news when it was announced, it would take a few months before much happened. RCA were unable to get Elvis into the studio immediately, so, re-released all six of the Sun singles, which they had also purchased as part of the deal.

Eventually, they got their new signing into the studio and recorded "Heartbreak Hotel", released as a single on January 27 1956. It went straight to the top of the charts! Parker also booked Elvis on CBS's 'Stage Show'. The ensuing exposure he received on national television introduced rockabilly to its widest audience yet and, like fire to kindling, there was no stopping its spread.

Other independent and major record companies alike took notice. They almost collectively decided that they too should look for an 'Elvis'. They swooped to sign up any artists who sang even vaguely similarly to Elvis, and in many cases whether they could sing or not! A bona fide musical feeding frenzy ensued, with record executives and studio bigwigs falling over themselves to capitalise on this musical trend now sweeping the nation, but ultimately playing a big part in rockabilly's eventual downfall.

The record companies had all recognised a change in music, albeit a little late; the way youngsters were suddenly interested in music and were creating a movement, a venture into a new sound. Now they decided that they needed a piece of the action. For the thousands of other performers who were playing similar music, but weren't sure how they could use this strange, up-tempo hillbilly sound, this was fantastic news. Suddenly they had a chance to record with a label, major or otherwise. In retrospect, what Elvis had done with the help of Sam Phillips, was to open that door for other young musicians. They saw this window of opportunity and the record companies, sensing a quick profit, were more than ready to take them on in the hope that they might be another Elvis. So, whilst Elvis' musical ability (he only played two or three chords) has over the years, been questioned, there can be no doubt that he perhaps unwittingly, opened the door for those that followed.

Elvis' sale also allowed Sam Phillips to explore a host of performers who had been begging for a chance. His Sun label would introduce to the world; Carl Perkins, Roy Orbison, Johnny Cash, and Billy Lee Riley, amongst others. What he DID find was one particularly special performer in the shape of Jerry Lee Lewis from Ferriday, Louisiana. He had arrived with his Father at the Sun studios apparently having sold a lorry load of eggs to afford to make the trip, and essentially insisted on playing for Sam Phillips. But Sam Phillips had been out of town, and the recording was made by Jack Clement, the studio engineer. When Phillips returned and heard the recording he got Jerry Lee back into the studio as fast as he could.

The things that this boy could do with the piano, would set the world alight. Yes, he had sold the contract of Elvis, who represented the beating heart of this new sound, because Sam Phillips knew that unless he did, Sun Records would have probably shut down. He recognised that, whilst he had all these other performers, they didn't, apart from Jerry Lee Lewis, have the same impact as Elvis did. They didn't turn ladies knees to jelly every time they performed and they didn't send the kids crazy. Deep in his heart, Sam Phillips had found a goldmine in Elvis and had let it go. In Jerry Lee Lewis, he had found another dynamic performerthat would in a very short time, make an even bigger impact, but not in any way that could have been predicted.

Jerry Lee's first big record was "Whole lotta shakin' going on", which included more than a spoonful of innuendo and once released, the kids went crazy for it. But, almost immediately, most radio stations banned it outright because of it's suggestive lyrics. Sam Phillips was apoplectic, he had a stockroom full of the records and no orders. To combat the problem, Sam asked his brother Jud to come and help out. Jud was excellent at selling and promoting, and decided to take Jerry Lee to New York and try to get him on a TV Show. Ed Sullivan refused to even meet him, but Steve Allen, seeing his chance to get one up on Sullivan, put Jerry Lee on, and the impact was almost instantaneous. Within a week, bans were dropped, orders returned and the pressing plants went into overdrive to try and satisfy the demand for a record that at it's height, was selling 50,000 copies a week!

Other record companies who saw the need to match RCA and acquire their own 'Elvis' introduced Mac Curtis, Ronnie Dawson, Gene Vincent, Johnny Burnette and his band, Eddie Cochran, Buddy Holly and many more. Whilst few of them were as successful as Elvis, at least they were getting recorded and released on vinyl, even if, for many of them, it turned out that it was only one or two records that were ever released.

Elvis started the ball rolling, and it was gathering speed as the music we now call rockabilly began to burn brightly. Whilst Elvis was creating waves in Memphis, other waves were being generated elsewhere, and all of these things would after a very short time indeed merge together to create what we now call rock 'n' roll.

In the north, there was the result of the great migrant surge from the south. Black families had travelled north to cities where they found work and began to settle down. Other blacks returning from the war were already there. There were a lot of gospel groups around, but one of the best talents to emerge was Sister Rosetta Tharpe. She was essentially a gospel singer, mixed in with the voice of a blues shouter, and had an uncanny talent with a guitar. Her music was powerful and influential; indeed, Ronnie Wood of The Rolling Stones cited her as a huge influence on his guitar playing. She was voted in a poll as being not only one of the best female guitarists of all time, but was also in the top ten of ALL guitarists. Then there were the Bluesmen, people like Ike Turner, Sticks McGhee, BB King, Big Joe Turner, Fats Domino, BB King, Howlin' Wolf, Lightening Hopkins, Amos Milburn and others, all of whom were making great rhythm and blues music and had been doing so for some time. Fats Domino when asked, said he didn't know what all the fuss was about as he had been playing this rock n' roll stuff for years!. And whilst some of them were based in New Orleans, they recorded for northern based labels such as Chess, based in Chicago. Chess, run by Lester, Marshall and Phil Chess was an important label for many of these black R n' B artists, as well as two performers who defied categorization; Bo Diddley, with his shuffling guitar rhythm and Chuck Berry with his duck walk.

A by-product of R&B was doo wop. Black teenagers would form themselves into groups, and because they had no money for instruments and were often not targeted by record companies, they would meet in their neighbourhoods, sometimes gathering beneath street lights and sing. They learnt to sing in close harmony, and without instrumentation, so would create their own, using their voices. One group member would take the lead (hence the term 'lead singer'), whilst others would lend backing vocals, often with a deep bass line. This music became known as doo wop, after the sound of the backing singers. And they, along with R&B, came to the notice of one particular radio disk jockey - his name was Alan Freed.

Alan Freed was without doubt a phenomenon. He was a DJ at WJW in Cleveland, Ohio, and had been playing some of the raunchiest R&B under the name of "Moondog" on his late-night show. He would howl and yell into the microphone to a small but growing audience that identified with him and the music. He was noticed by Leo Mintz, who owned one of the biggest record stores in Cleveland. Mintz and Leo Platt, a local booking agent and promoter, got together with Freed to stage a dance to be billed as the Moondog Coronation Ball. What happened next entered into the annuls of music history.

The Coronation Ball was to be held on March 21, 1952, at the Cleveland Arena. Freed expressed concern that there might not be enough people turning up, and he might be out of pocket. In the event, quite the opposite happened. Thousands turned up, many of them without tickets, and as they surged into the building, joining those already there, chaos ensued. The police and the fire brigade attempted unsuccessfully to control the crowd, and eventually the Chief of Police had no option other than to cancel the event there and then. The recriminations afterwards were widespread and vociferous. According to the press some 25,000 people turned up, although this figure is speculative. In reality, there were about 9,000 tickets sold, and some 12–14,000 without tickets. Numbers are, however, confusing. Freed, in his defence, said that everything was fine until an estimated 7,000 stormed the doors. The white city authorities blamed Freed for encouraging a mob of blacks to gather in such numbers, but the black community blamed Freed and the organisers for using the black performers in what they saw as derogatory exploitation of the blacks.

The upper and middle class within the black community, did not like what they perceived as the raw and often obscene nature of R&B, describing it as "gutbucket blues". Instead, they preferred to see more cultural events to try and break the racial stereotypes which the whites often portrayed of the blacks. The night following the Cleveland Arena fiasco, Freed urged his listeners to send in their requests with messages of support for him and the station, threatening to pull the show from the air if he didn't receive this vote of confidence. He needn't have worried; the show was overwhelmed by messages of support and the switchboards jammed.

Pretty soon tapes of Freed's programme began to air in the New York City area over station WNJR

1430 (now WNSW) in Newark, New Jersey. In July 1954, following his success on the air in Cleveland, Freed moved to WINS in New York City. His radio show there played almost exclusive R&B music. His on-air manner was energetic, he would shout and thump his fist on the console, often urging his listeners to scream out of the window where they lived, in stark contrast to many contemporary radio presenters of traditional pop music, who tended to sound more subdued and low-key in manner. He addressed his listeners as if they were all part of a make-believe kingdom of hipsters, united in their love for black music. He also began popularizing the phrase "rock and roll" to describe the music he played. Some histories say that Freed 'invented' the term "rock 'n' roll", but that is stretching the truth too far. It would, however, be fair to say that, if nothing else, he will be remembered as the man that adopted the term 'rock 'n' roll', and bought it into mainstream usage.

Alan Freed

Of course, Freed wasn't the first white man to play black rhythm and blues on a radio station. That honour falls to a couple of southern based disk jockeys who had been doing it since the end of the war. In Nashville a 50,000 watt station, WLAC, boasted presenters "Daddy" Gene Nobles and John Richbourg. Both were white men who regularly played 'jump band Jazz', with Richbourg having joined Nobles just after the war. Both noted that there was an upsurge of requests for black music, and they, with the authorisation of their station, catered to these requests. In doing so, they demonstrated that it was commercially viable to programme this music. It may be something of a surprise to the reader that they managed to get away with this in the notoriously racial south.

As the popularity of their shows increased, the station developed and was eventually, with the help of that powerful 50,000-watt transmitter, broadcasting as far north as Canada! They weren't the only ones though. In Memphis, radio station WDIA lost so much money by trying similar programming aimed at whites, that after just a year they switched their focus to targeting just the black population of the area, and became an almost instant success. Bill Gordon claimed to be the first white man to play rhythm and blues on the radio on WMPS in Memphis from around 1946 through to 1950, but in 1948 Hunter Hancock disputed the claim whilst broadcasting for KFVD in Los Angeles. And there were many more.

So, whilst Alan Freed was probably not consciously aware of these pioneers, the radio stations in the north certainly were, but at the time didn't consider playing such music was feasible in their part of America. They were soon to change their minds, however. As the great migration of the blacks to the north gathered pace, it meant that there was, almost overnight a large black audience to be targeted. Alan Freed would go on to create a huge listening audience, and also to organise more concerts in the same manner as the Cleveland Arena one, but without the chaos. However, he did create chaos on air. On July 11th, 1955, he was playing "Moondog Symphony", a very strange piece, during which a dog is heard to emit a mournful howl. Freed, playing to his audience, attempted to playfully silence the dog, by saying, "come on now Moondog, please stop howling or you'll wake up the neighbours!" Suddenly the station switchboard was inundated with listeners phoning in, reacting to Freed and the dog. Freed very quickly established the name, 'Moondog', and built the show around it, calling his listeners "Moondoggers", and would howl through an open microphone, calling his listeners to follow suit - often they did, opening windows and howling, to the confusion and consternation of any adults nearby!

With the success of his radio show, Freed decided once again to stage live concerts. He would feature live performances with names such as Fats Domino, Chuck Berry, The Moonglows, The Platters, the Drifters and many of the doo wop and other groups who jumped at the chance to perform in front of an audience and get noticed. The shows were attended by thousands of black and white kids, mixing in and enjoying the music. This was an alarming aspect for the authorities, apart from the traffic jams the events caused. The fact that black and white teenagers were openly mixing together was a huge shock, and the authorities and music establishment vowed to do all they could to stop Freed and his rock 'n' roll. But, pretty soon, other radio stations began playing this new rock n' roll, employing suitably hip disk jockeys to present the music, as mentioned, they were characters and some of them went completely over the top! There are numerous stories of a disk jockey playing a record over and over again, locking themselves into their studio to play a particular record continuously, much to the consternation of radio station owners and their sponsors, but the kids lapped it up!

It is poignant at this time to mention an ongoing spat between ASCAP (American Society of Composers, Authors and Publishers), founded in 1914, and BMI (Broadcast Music Incorporated), founded in 1939. Officially, ASCAP were there to protect their members from unauthorised broadcasting of their work. Unofficially, they operated a cartel, and were extremely strict about whom they granted membership to. In 1923 they sued the broadcasting media (i.e. radio stations), who hitherto had not paid any royalties to the authors, composers or performers, whose records they played. The American court found in favour of ASCAP, and from then on, radio stations were obliged to pay performance royalties to the copyright holders. However, in 1937 ASCAP proposed that broadcasters' emoluments be increased to 100%, which incensed the broadcasters, who then formed BMI (Broadcast music Incorporated). The relationship was never a happy one, and in 1953 ASCAP filed a $150 million lawsuit against BMI, who they claimed were guilty of monopolistic practices. ASCAP also began targeting DJ's like Alan Freed, who they accused of corrupting the nation's morals by playing R&B records, such as "It ain't the meat, it's the motion" by The Swallows, "Sixty minute man" by The Dominos, and The Ravens' "Rock me all night long", all of which were seen as, at best risqué, and at worst downright explicit. BMI, faced with the weight of ASCAP and other organisations such as religious groups, teachers and parents and many more, eventually conceded, and they bought in rules that forbade blatantly pornographic lyrics. The lawsuit dragged on and on, and had much to do with the instigation of the Payola Investigation, but more of that later.

Rock n' roll shocked the establishment and just when they thought it couldn't get any worse, they were stopped in their tracks, at least temporarily, by a white hillbilly performer, also out of Cleveland, by the name of Bill Haley. Bill Haley had been playing with a variety of country, hillbilly and Western swing bands, but had only rarely featured as the lead singer or front man. He formed his own band, and on the basis that he had noticed an increase in white kids listening to and buying black R&B records, began experimenting with tunes such as the "ABC boogie", "Razzle dazzle", "Dim dim the lights". All these tunes were released on the small Essex label and, whilst they weren't hits, they were in fact the most authentic of all Haley and his group's output.

They also became noticed and the band, by now called Bill Haley and the Comets, began to get talked about by the kids. In 1954 Haley recorded "Rock Around the Clock". Initially it was a moderate success, peaking at number 23 on the Billboard pop singles chart and staying on the charts for a few weeks. "Rock Around the Clock" was re-released when it appeared as the theme song of the 1955 film Blackboard Jungle. It soared to the top of the American Billboard chart for eight weeks. The kids went wild! It reached number 1 across the USA and much of Europe. Haley soon had another worldwide hit with "Shake, Rattle and Roll", another rhythm and blues cover, in this case from Big Joe Turner, after he'd cleaned up the original lyrics, which, in true R&B style, were sensationally risqué. It went on to sell a million copies, and was the first rock 'n' roll song to enter the British singles charts in December 1954, becoming a gold record. He retained elements of the original (which was slow blues), but sped it up with some country music aspects into the song (specifically, Western swing).

Suddenly Bill Haley was 'the man'. Unfortunately, Haley had an image problem. He was slightly overweight, balding and was in his thirties. Hardly the image of a wild rock 'n' roller by any stretch of the imagination. The teenagers, although they loved the music, accused him of being a 'square' trying to be a 'cat'. Within three months Elvis came to national prominence, and he WAS the real deal! He was tall, sultry, and the perfect icon for this wild new music. Bill Haley knew the game was up, as he realised that he couldn't compete with this good-looking young man. However, Haley was comfortable in the knowledge that, whilst he may not have been the idol the teenagers were looking for, he had certainly been the first white performer to openly play and record rock 'n' roll. And his music was important in launching the music known as "rock and roll" to a wider audience.

Bill Haley

Rock 'n' roll exploded onto a largely unsuspecting American market. It was, for a while, everywhere, and it was social chaos. Quite apart from the music, the teenagers adopted, for the first time, their own styles of dress, which included denim jeans, T-shirts (actually a garment first employed by the US Navy for their sailors), Penny Loafer shoes (so called because a penny could be stored in a flap on the top of the shoe), and it all came with an attitude and a language of their own. At one time, the authorities even tried to ban denim jeans, which they had associated with teenage hoodlums. Teenagers at schools were disciplined for wearing tight pencil skirt dresses, chewing gum, and all the time tapping their toes to this outrageous noise that the kids called rock 'n' roll.

The older generation didn't understand, and it's not surprising when performers like Little Richard were screaming "A wop bop a lop bop a lop bam boom"! Bill Haley was urging them to "Rock around the clock" or to "Rip it up", Jerry Lee Lewis was as wild as they come, singing about "Great balls of fire!" and Buddy Holly was telling everyone he was going to rock around with Ollie Vee! What did it all mean? And why can't these kids talk properly? They call each other cat, call outsiders 'Daddy Oh', and tell us to 'dig the beat'! And they stayed out until all hours of the night, getting up to Lord knows what. They turned ordinary cars into hot rods, would drag race around the streets, stage 'chicken runs', and generally run amok. What was it all about!? Parents, the establishment and the church were appalled, and felt like they were under siege. Their world had gone crazy man crazy!

CHAPTER FIVE
The Establishment Fights Back

The original rockabilly and rock 'n' roll music of the 1950's enjoyed unprecedented influence when it first exploded into public consciousness, and the establishment hated it! It was new, it was different, and quite part from the fact it encouraged black and whites to mix, the performers were outrageous! Whilst Elvis was the one that made the breakthrough, he might also be partly responsible for its demise. He would shock middle class America and the older generation by gyrating his hips and shaking his leg in a manner popularised by striptease and burlesque artists. He had enjoyed a brief affair with a stripper, Stormy Tempest, and without doubt would have learned a few moves. Elvis' debut on *The Ed Sullivan Show* on September 9, 1956, drew an estimated 82% of the American viewing public (54 million people), who watched him sing "Don't Be Cruel" and "Love Me Tender". But it was his performance of "Hound Dog", where he bumped, wiggled and gyrated - shocking parents, middle class America and elder statesmen so much that it was ordered he be filmed only from the waist up, and watched by police to determine whether it was unnecessarily lewd or obscene! (It wasn't). Elvis' music was banned in the Soviet Union under the premise that the music was a CIA plot designed to undermine the morals of their children! Much the same argument was put forward in America, but for the different reason that Elvis, who owned a pink Cadillac, must be a communist!

Johnny Burnette and the rock n' roll trio were far wilder on stage Chuck Berry introduced the world to something called 'the duck walk', whilst he played guitar (a move that ACDC's Angus Young still uses today!), there was Bo Diddley with his unique guitars and rhythms who was asked not to play a certain song on the Ed Sullivan show, went ahead and did it anyway, Johnny Carroll and his band were frenetic and the way he shook whilst singing, surely he had something wrong with him? It's no wonder America, who were used to the likes of Perry Como and Frank Sinatra, loathed it, and in very short, began to try and subdue and control it.

The music was labelled 'jungle music' by the church, who were outraged and made sure to let everyone know it as often as possible. There were televised sermons, where preachers laid siege to the music and the impact it had on young minds. Some radio stations, traditionally steeped in jazz and swing, banned rock 'n' roll overtly and dramatically, smashing records on TV and air, another prominent Jazz musician described this new music as "...the blues without the music". Rock 'n' roll was under attack from all sides.

In 1954, a Michigan Congressman had introduced a house bill to prohibit the mailing of any "pornographic" recordings. A bright spark took advantage and labelled certain records as having a "pornographic quality", thus enabling many records to be stopped from being distributed. In Memphis, police confiscated boxes and boxes of The Drifters' "Honey Love" before they could be loaded onto lorries that would have distributed them!

In Ohio, dancing to rock 'n' roll records by anyone under the age of 18 was banned, whilst in New York, a Colombia record executive hosted a serious discussion, live on CBS, to determine whether anyone who enjoyed rock 'n' roll might be in need of psychiatric help, and also what negative effects it had on young minds!

Chuck Berry had been jailed for supposedly transporting a prostitute across a state line, an allegation he always denied, and Little Richard was so obviously camp, he even wore make up, so that the church would question his morals and the effect on children. Whilst on tour in Australia, Little Richard saw a plane's engine explode, which he took as a sign from God, so he threw all his (costume) jewellery out of the window of the train he was on, and gave up performing rock 'n' roll, ironically to become a preacher.

Johnny Burnette and the Rock 'n' Roll Trio often came off stage minus their trousers and shirts, as the teenagers in the audiences went wild. As we will see, Alan Freed's career (and some claim his life) would be ruined in the Payola scandals, proving, as far as the establishment were concerned, that the people involved in rock 'n' roll were just no good. And it wasn't just in America... rock 'n' roll frenzy had spread across the world.

In Germany, where Bill Haley and the Comets were playing, the audience became so frenzied that they smashed up every seat in the place, and it was nearly a full-scale riot. Jerry Lee Lewis, by now the hottest name at Sun Records, whose stage act was far wilder than many of them, joined in.

He would scream and shout, his long hair out of control, and would not be upstaged by anyone. Once, it was claimed, when booked as second on the bill to Chuck Berry, he set fire to his piano, stomped off stage and said to the waiting Berry "follow that!" His first hit, "Whole Lotta Shakin'" was initially banned (although it had sold over 100,000 copies, and would go on to sell millions!).

But in 1958, he had travelled on tour to England, where it was discovered by a journalist that he was married to his 13-year-old cousin, Myra. In fact, she was 15, but the British press soon saw through that; not that a couple of years made any difference. It was not the best thing to reveal to a deeply conservative Britain!

His tour lasted just four dates before he scuttled back to the USA, allegedly telling reporters at the airport that if anyone didn't like it, they could "fuck off"! In the US he faced further moral outrage, and it would take him ten years to recover his name.

Jerry Lee Lewis

As we have said, the American establishment hated rock 'n' roll, and its impact was felt throughout American society. The establishment was determined to get rid of it by any means, fair or foul. Even established performers were appalled by rock 'n' roll. Frank Sinatra, described rock 'n' roll as "..the most brutal, ugly, degenerate, vicious form of expression it has been my misfortune to hear..".

But why had it happened? The first wave of rock 'n' roll arrived just as segregationists were tightening laws in response to the civil rights movement. There were real fears of race mixing, that young black and white kids would get together over this music, with its rhythmic, primitive, sensuous beat. Rock 'n' roll had a trans formative effect because it encouraged younger people to break out of the more conservative American mold.

America at this time, was experiencing real racial tensions. The idea of abolishing segregation was new and very much in its infancy. On May 17, 1954, the US. Supreme Court ruled in the case *Brown*

v *Board of Education of Topeka,* that racial segregation in public schools was unconstitutional.
The decision effectively overturned the separate
but equal ruling of *Plessy* v. *Ferguson* (1896),
which had allowed the so called 'Jim Crow' laws
(see Chapter 2), that mandated separate public
facilities for white and black Americans to prevail
throughout the South during the first half of the
20th century.

While the *Brown* ruling applied only to schools,
it implied that segregation in other public facilities was unconstitutional as well. This, in theory,
meant that black children could attend, mix and
be educated on an equal basis. In reality this was,
not surprisingly, openly opposed in the Southern
States, and defied in most Northern states. And,
of course, there was also the infamous Rosa Parks
incident.

On December 1, 1955, African American civil
rights activist Rosa Parks refused to give up her
seat on a public bus to a white passenger. Her
subsequent arrest initiated a sustained bus boycott in Montgomery, Alabama. The protest
began on December 5, led by Martin Luther King
Junior, then a young, local pastor, and was so successful that it was extended indefinitely. In the
ensuing months, protesters faced threats, arrests,
and termination from their jobs. Nonetheless, the
boycott continued for more than a year. Finally,
the Supreme Court upheld a lower court's ruling
that segregated seating was unconstitutional, and
the federal decision went into effect on December
20, 1956.

In September 1957, nine African American students attended their first day at Little Rock Central High School, whose entire student population had until that point, been white. 'The Little Rock Nine', as they came to be called, encountered a large white mob and soldiers from the Arkansas National Guard (sent by Arkansas Governor, Orval Eugene Faubus) blocking the entrance of the school. For the next 18 days President Dwight D. Eisenhower, Governor Faubus, and Little Rock's mayor, Woodrow Mann, discussed the situation. The Little Rock Nine returned on September 23, but were met with violence. The students were sent home, and returned on September 25, protected by US soldiers. Although the students were continually harassed, eight of the nine completed the academic year. The entire confrontation drew international attention, not only to civil rights in the United States, but also to the struggle between federal and state power. Such issues continued throughout the 1950's and 1960's, right up to the assassination of Malcolm X, the Watts riots in 1965, the founding of the black panther movement in 1966, and the assassination of Martin Luther King Junior in 1968.

The original declaration of emancipation devised and declared by Abraham Lincoln on *September 22, 1862,* was ratified by the thirteenth amendment in 1864 and 1865, effectively freeing the slaves in the Confederate states of the south. But they were treated just as badly in the northern states as they were in the southern. In the southern states, any form of race mixing was vehemently and openly opposed, and there were plenty of reports of attacks by white supremacists, led and encouraged by groups such as the Ku Klux Klan. In a few notorious cases, black people were actually murdered by Klan members and their supporters, and whilst the perpetrators were dragged into court and charged, very few of them were convicted, as it was generally accepted that no court, especially in the south, would convict a white American of murder, when the victim was black. It is therefore not difficult to conclude that by the 1950's, America had essentially never moved on, and was inherently racist.

It was against this backdrop that rockabilly and rock 'n' roll music emerged, encouraging black and white teenagers to mix. It became, almost by accident, instrumental in implementing and supporting the civil rights movements, and their struggle to achieve equality. At venues, black groups faced ridiculous rules from promoters, often supported and enforced by the local police force. For instance, one night The Flamingos' bus pulled up to a concert hall in Birmingham, Alabama, to find a row of 30 to 50 police officers holding rifles and billy clubs waiting for them. The cops escorted the six-members of the doo-wop group to the dressing room and gave strict instructions; as black performers, that they were only to make eye contact with black fans, who were confined to the balcony, and not with whites down below! Anyone who has ever performed on a stage will know that it is almost impossible to focus so high up, without looking as though you were either taking some pretty strong drugs or searching for invading aliens from outer space!

Entertainers throughout the country were forced to participate in similar crowd separation rituals. Venues could be unofficially classified black or white. For example; Police and promoters physically separated the audiences. Sometimes, blacks were in the balcony and whites in the stalls, sometimes the other way around. At other times, a painted line ran down the centre of the theatre or a rope divided the audience. In 1955, Chuck Berry performed in Jacksonville, Florida, and recalled in his autobiography;

"...Just before they were to open the doors for the spectators, four of the maintenance guys came out and roped off the auditorium with white window cord. They looped and tied it to each seat down the centre aisle, making it an off-limits zone that neither coloured nor whites could tread."

Berry also wrote that he once showed up for a Knoxville, Tennessee, concert only to find a group of white men had replaced him with a local cover band. One of the promoters in charge, without any sense of impropriety, said;

"It's a country dance, and we had no idea that 'Maybellene' was recorded by a niggra man."

In 1957, cops interrupted a biracial jam session at New Orleans' Preservation Hall and arrested all the musicians. The judge told an assembled courthouse crowd, according to several who were in the public gallery;

"We don't want Yankees coming down to New Orleans mixing cream with our coffee."

The Coasters were climbing down from their tour bus when the promoter told them "Uh, we're looking for the Coasters band."The group replied, "We are the Coasters band."The man said, "I think they're white."

Hughes told him, "No, we're black."

One of the men standing around panicked.

"They ain't white!" he said. Let's get them out of here!"

The Coasters were returned to their bus and were escorted out of town in a hurry.

Jackie Wilson played a package show with several top singers in Little Rock, Arkansas. When he realised they were scheduled to play two shows, the first one for blacks, then the second for the whites, he pulled out of the second one. Local white residents, on hearing of this, brandished guns and chased Wilson's entourage out of town.

Buddy Holly and the Crickets were famously booked to play the Apollo Theatre in Harlem, a notorious black ghetto in New York. As the curtains opened, the audience gasped at the sight of four white performers. However, Buddy was known for his way of getting to an audience, and the band launched into "Rock around with Ollie Vee", and within a few seconds, the black audience was going as wild as they would have done for a favourite black band.

The teenagers had begun to resist segregation; rock 'n' roll shows became so boisterously and overtly biracial that it was sometimes impossible for officials to fully segregate them. Some recall the cops simply throwing up their hands and giving up. Young whites and blacks always seemed to find ways to breach the separation.

After the first intermission, at which the black and white kids were all dancing together, one performer said"I just kept playing my music and the kids kept coming... They were rebelling through dance; through a beat I'd created... They start realizing we're all human".

Some courageous musicians, black and white, contributed to concert desegregation, which continued in some places, even after it was outlawed in 1964.

The emergence of rock 'n' roll music into mainstream consciousness, and the genuine moral panic which ensued, are significant due to the fact that it was one of the first, if not the only, major music genre of the time, to take direct influence from African-American styles of music. These African-American roots of rockabilly music, and its evolution into the wider-known rock 'n' roll genre, would play a key role in its widespread popularity, and the establishment's opposition to it.

Additionally, with cities being home to a mix of blacks and whites living within the same environment, it was obvious that the styles of music between the two were beginning to feed off each other, which was the start of major race mixing within music.

Alan Freed became a prime target for the authorities. The problem with Alan Freed was that he
simply couldn't be told what to do, and hated
authority. If he was told he couldn't do something
on air, he did it. In 1958, Freed faced controversy
in Boston when he told the audience, "It looks like
the Boston police don't want you to have a good
time."

As a result, Freed was arrested and charged with
inciting a riot, and was fired from his job at WINS.
Freed's career was further significantly affected
when it was shown that he HAD, despite earlier
denials, accepted payola (payments from record
companies to play specific records), which was
highly controversial at the time. It is ironic that
originally the Payola investigations had originally
focused on TV game shows, where accusations
had emerged that the shows quiz format were
fixed. Almost by accident, the focus shifted to
music, which suited the American establishment.
Essentially, the idea was that they accused certain
disk jockeys of accepting bribes to falsely promote
the music. While working at WABC (AM), Freed
refused to sign a statement for the FCC stating
that he never received bribes. In 1960, payola was
made illegal. But the investigation dragged on for
another two years until, in December 1962, after
being charged on multiple counts of commercial
bribery, Freed pleaded guilty to two counts and
was fined $300 and given a suspended sentence.
The toll on Freed personally, however, had been
taken, along with copious amounts of alcohol, and
he rarely worked after that, passing away in 1965.

All this controversy was caused by the American establishment's failure to understand, or adapt to, changes in society that had allowed rockabilly and rock 'n' roll to emerge, or indeed how to deal with it. So, they tried to destroy it and failed. For instance, Dick Clark, a rock 'n' roll disk jockey also named in the payola scandal, testified before the committee, but avoided repercussions, partially due to the fact that he had divested his ownership interest in music-industry holdings, so, yes, he had accepted payments, but he was essentially paying himself! But Dick was a good, clean cut, young man, morally acceptable to the establishment. He also gave evidence, which, whilst none of it was against Alan Freed, certainly didn't help or support him. What the establishment and the record companies were scared of, were the social implications of allowing racial integration. Worse still, they had no control over it. Segregation was directly threatened by this music, and they felt that they desperately had to try and gain some control. Following the payola scandal, and the much-exaggerated harm and influence of rock 'n' roll, they more or less had control back. But they were too late. By the time the Payola investigation had concluded, rock 'n' roll had already changed beyond all recognition.

The 1956 original version of rock 'n' roll had been replaced by 1958, into a manufactured, sugar coated and very much watered-down version, a parody of itself, if you will, aided and abetted by Dick Clark's 'American Bandstand' TV Show, where wholesome, clean cut kids would be seen dancing in the studio. The music was performed by manufactured performers such as Frankie Avalon, Fabian, Paul Anka, Tommy Sands and others, described by Jerry Lee Lewis as "drips". None of them were a patch on the likes of Gene Vincent, Eddie Cochran or Lewis himself. Gone was the raw excitement, edginess and spontaneity of rockabilly and rock 'n' roll. It was no longer dangerous. To some extent, this was the music industry protecting itself. Dick Clark and the record companies realised that the establishment was pulling out all the stops in trying to take control, so they acted before they were pushed, Clark presenting his tv shows to show that not all teenagers were leather jacketed hoodlums, and the record companies also changed the type of performer that had pioneered rock n' roll.

No longer were record companies looking for young rockabilly rebels. Rock 'n' roll had taken them as much by surprise as anyone else and, as we have seen, even the established music industry to some extent hated it. Instead, therefore, they concentrated on finding good, clean-cut boys, who were not only good looking and cool, but would deliver pleasant and safe music in a way that was acceptable to everyone. It was almost as if music had gone back to the harmless state of the big bands and crooners. However, in a curious way, none of these manufactured pretty boys lasted very long. Many of them were 'one hit wonders'. It's ironic that the original, raw and dangerous rockabilly rebels outlasted them by decades, and are still revered to this day!

Of the white performers left unscathed by these changes, many returned to straight country music, were incorporated into it, or become a minority offshoot, a sort of distant cousin, or just retired. There were very few that continued to perform rockabilly or rock 'n' roll, although notably Wanda Jackson, Ronnie Dawson and Carl Perkins continued to record some, but it was largely ignored. They also recorded country material as well. Of course, they still played and occasionally turned up as guests on TV programmes, but were no longer front-page news, and were regarded as some sort of novelty attraction. In just a few short years all trace of rockabilly had disappeared, and original rock 'n' roll was very much marginalised; it had changed and mutated through various phases, which continued through the 1960's and are ongoing to this day.

Black R&B music had also been accepted into the mainstream, but became a different animal with a different name. By the early 1960's, they first began calling it soul. Performers like Sam Cooke, Ivory Joe Hunter, James Brown and Jackie Wilson, rather than Howling Wolf, Hank Ballard and Lightening Hopkins, were now the household names. Soul music and its offspring, Tamla Motown, later evolved and became known as disco, and later, rap music, but all of it had its roots in the black rhythm and blues of the 1950's.

In contrast to America, rock 'n' roll did not at first, get across the pond directly to the UK or Europe. But Britain, for instance, had a huge merchant fleet that travelled worldwide, and the seamen on board would have heard the music and seen what was going on. Pretty soon these young men were smitten, and would return to British ports laden with stories of this musical revolution, as well as records, and the word got out. Soon there was an army of youngsters across the European continent that also wanted to join in. And because they were remote from the source, they were perhaps even more enthusiastic than their American counterparts.

The British music industry, steeped in jazz and classical orchestra music, like the American music industry at first, didn't understand what all the fuss was about. They thought it was just an American craze that would soon die out. Some rock 'n' roll and R&B, and even a smattering of rockabilly recordings, were issued in Great Britain.

It was included on many record company catalogues, but not promoted and as far as chart entries were concerned, they were few and far between. To buy it, you had to order the records because they weren't on direct sale in the shops. You just had to be in the know. Radio Luxemburg, however, provided a steady source of listening, but the BBC were having none of it, at least not to begin with.

Rock 'n' roll in Great Britain was, at first, only accessible in the mainstream, from music based teen TV shows, such as 'Boy Meets Girl', 'The Six Five Special' and 'Oh Boy'. But even here, there were perhaps just one or two real rock 'n' rollers played on disc with a troupe of dancers trotting around to the music. Most of the shows featured established artists, often trying in an unconvincing way, to be hip with the teenagers! It was Jack Goode who produced probably the best TV Show in 'Oh Boy'! He actually got the British rock 'n' roll stars to appear, even managing to get Eddie Cochran and Gene Vincent onto the show.

American performers, when they visited Europe, found the audiences were fanatical. Gene Vincent is a good case in point. He had hit the heights with 'Be Bop a Lula', which reached No 7 in America, but he never really came close to that top ten success again until he reached Europe.

Britain had established its own rock 'n' roll scene, featuring the likes of Billy Fury, Cliff Richard, Marty Wilde, Tommy Steele, Don Lang and his Frantic Five, Johnny Kidd and the Pirates, Vince Eager and Vince Taylor. They were later augmented by adopted imports, Gene Vincent and Eddie Cochran. Although much maligned as 'watered down rock 'n' roll', a lot of it was actually pretty good. During its heyday in Britain, rock 'n' roll caused as much, if not more, of a sensation than in America.

Officially, rock 'n' roll arrived in Britain in 1954 with the release of Bill Haley's 'Rock around the Clock', closely followed by Elvis' 'Heartbreak Hotel'. The British youth went wild for it. Britain, though, did not have the same racial tensions going on in the background, but even so, rock 'n' roll in Britain was still banned from many clubs, pubs and social halls, as were several films, such as "Blackboard Jungle" and "The Wild One", loosely based on the Hollister riots (which we discussed in Chapter One). Following the screening of the first blatant rock 'n' roll film, "Rock around the Clock", in the Elephant and Castle region of South London, rock 'n' roll was banned or had severe restrictions put upon it after a riot involving the Teddy Boys.

It is worth discussing the cult of the Teddy Boys at this point. Whilst America was having a post war ball, Britain was suffering from severe austerity. From this rationing and shortage of almost all luxuries, came the spivs... people that would 'acquire' goods from nefarious sources, and sell them to whoever had any money at inflated prices. However, most of these people were basically nothing more than petty criminals, and normally a little older. Just as teenagers in the USA found freedom of expression, so too in Britain, the younger population did the same, especially from the working class. There is evidence that British Army officers, mostly from the Guards Regiments, began to affect pseudo-Edwardian fashions, wearing long coats with velvet collars, combined with crepe soled chukka boots, first introduced to the British army for their operations in the desert campaigns. However, as soon as working-class youths began to adopt the same fashions, the Guards officers dropped the practice quickly.

The Teddy Boys movement was said to have originated in South London's Elephant and Castle area, but there is in fact evidence that much the same idea was also beginning in other places, like Manchester and Birmingham.

The Edwardians or Teds, as they became known, were not particularly deep thinkers; they knew they wanted to rebel, they knew that they didn't wish to be seen as part of the establishment. They wanted something different. No high and mighty ideals, they simply wanted to enjoy themselves on their own terms. When they first emerged, swing music and jazz was the only music available, but when, in 1954, rock 'n' roll hit Britain, they quickly adopted it as their music. Today, they are viewed through rose tinted spectacles, as the saying goes, but, let's be honest, original Teddy Boys were not the sort of people that you took to visit your girlfriend's mother! Forget the manufactured image the media created later in the 1950's, these were nasty, vicious thugs who would roam the streets in large gangs. Rival gangs would fight each other, armed with flick knives (The weapon of choice), chains, coshes, choppers and in a few cases, guns which were still legal then.

Teddy Boys were the first totally unique youth cult in Great Britain, and were responsible for at least four murders and innumerable assaults and woundings. Their violence and behaviour, at its worst, was far worse than the later mods, rockers and skinheads that followed in the 1960's and 1970's. Of course, media reports of what they did were often exaggerated, but they were still a major source of concern to the establishment, for whom lawlessness and rock 'n' roll music went hand in hand. So whilst America attacked the source...rock n' roll music, the British establishment attacked the Teddy boys, eventually winning by watering them down. By the late 1950's and early 1960's, holiday camps such as Butlins and Pontins, would have amongst their entertainments, events such as "The best dressed Teddy" competition, and they rarely played any rock n' roll at their dances, and if it was included, it was played by the campsite resident band, more often than not, a jazz/swing band with no feel for the music.

But in purely musical terms, rock 'n' roll in Britain was certainly as vibrant as it was in America, and it was going strong until the early 1960's. Music and fashion trends change very quickly, and with the emergence of The Dave Clark Five, The Rolling Stones and The Beatles, amongst others, the unique British rock 'n' roll sound was effectively killed off. Whilst mainstream Britain flocked to see the bright new stars on the scene, there was a whole army of British rock 'n' roll fans who were forgotten, and spent most of the swinging 60's lurking, wishing and hoping that rock 'n' roll would return. They would have to wait nearly ten years.

CHAPTER SIX

Revival

America had forgotten about rock 'n' roll and rockabilly in their original forms from the early 1960's onwards, when they were besieged by a British invasion by The Dave Clark Five and then the Beatles.

After that, it was psychedelic music that swept in the generation of love and piece, listening to bands such as Canned heat, Jefferson Airplane and Ten years after. Until in the very late 1960's, strange noises emerged from overseas that a huge revival in rock n' roll interest was happening.

The word 'rockabilly' kept cropping up as well, but America hadn't used the word much in the 1950's, and certainly didn't recognise it in the 1970's, let alone link it to music. Mention to anyone in America in the 1970's about a rock 'n' roll festival, and they would have pointed you to a show featuring The Clovers, The Drifters, The Five Satins and other doo wop groups from the mid to late 1950's. Mention rockabilly and their eyes would glaze over and they would simply stare, wondering what you were talking about!

But there was some hope. The American rock 'n' roll revival movement received its initial impetus from nostalgia tour packages organized by one Richard Nader, the veteran Dick Clark, and other promoters, which featured original rock 'n' roll artists (albeit often with drastically altered line ups) such as The Coasters, The Drifters, Fats Domino, Little Richard, and Bill Haley and His Comets as well as a contemporary retro group, Sha Na Na. The New York-based Sha Na Na employed goofy stage antics, with an uncanny ability to perform carbon copy renditions of classic rock 'n' roll and R&B hits.

In fact, Sha Na Na had emerged from the Woodstock festival, a huge hippy music jamboree (of love and peace, maaan) where such luminaries as Janis Joplin, Jimi Hendrix, Santana, Creedence Clearwater Revival and others were booked to appear. Due to bad weather and a fairly unorganised schedule, Sha Na Na were booked late on in the process and were the only unsigned group to appear. Hitherto they had been playing in small clubs to indifferent and uninterested customers, and were simply happy to have been booked onto a paying gig (they received a cheque for Woodstock, which later bounced!)

Their moment of glory came as they bounded onto the stage clad in gold lamé suits, and pronounced "I got one thing to say to all you hippies out there... rock 'n' roll is here to stay!" They went down a storm and were soon signed to a record label on the back of their performance. Whilst they were originally perceived as a huge novelty act in America, they went on to record many albums, host their own TV Show, and inspired the formation of many more revival acts in the U.S.A.

The popularity of the American movement peaked with the release of the George Lucas film, American Graffiti, in 1972. The film was immense, and it resonated with many Americans, reminding them of their teenage years. It went on to become one of the top-grossing films of all time, and one of its stars, Ron Howard, joined the cast of the popular TV show, "Happy Days", starring Henry Winkler, who had also been in another retro based, cult film, "The Lords of the Flatbush". By the mid-1970s, however, record sales of rock 'n' roll reissues and retro releases had greatly declined as the American music industry turned its attention to other fads. Once again, mainstream America had seemingly fallen out of love with original rock 'n' roll. But there were a few small enclaves where there was a genuine love of the 1950's, rock 'n' roll, and later rockabilly music.

The slightly eccentric and gregarious Ronny Weiser was one. He had grown up in Europe, listening to his mother playing a variety of music, and in 1959, whilst in Italy, he saw Elvis in the film, "Loving you", and he caught the bug. He was 18 when his family returned to live in the U.S. At the time, there was the so-called 'summer of love' going on, with hippies lacing their hair with flowers and their bodies with psychedelic drugs. Ronnie wasn't interested, and instead began collecting 1950's rock 'n' roll records. Ronny had a beef. He was disgusted and disappointed that America had turned its back on rock 'n' roll, and formed the Hollywood rock 'n' roll fan club. He began to publish his own newsletter, to be sent to members, and with a not-so-subtle poke in the eye at Rolling Stone magazine he called it "Rollin' Rock"! His magazine took off, and he found it astonishing that most of the subscribers were British and European. He decided to put together and sell a limited edition 10" album made up of insanely rare rock 'n' roll tracks. Well, he nearly did. He realised that if he did this, the LP would be a bootleg, and carry an unwanted stigma with it. So, he formed Rollin' Rock Records, and began to track down the owners of some of the original record labels.

In almost every case, the record label owners were surprised and bewildered that anyone was actually interested in the music that they held, much less want to lease them. But Ronny had a feeling that he was right, and so it proved. The record sales were phenomenal and were mostly sold to the British and European market. Encouraged, Ronny repeated the exercise, and over the next few years continued to release sought after tracks on his Rollin' Rock label.

Dave Harris imported large numbers of Ronny Weiser's Rollin' Rock Records, and helped to organize the famous Rollin' Rock tour of 1977, introducing Ray Campi & His Rockabilly Rebels, Mac Curtis, and others which, according to the British press, spawned the whole Rockabilly Rebels and Hep Cats movement. What followed was a movement that gathered speed and soon exploded onto the UK and European music scenes.

As Ronny Weiser was doing his thing in the U.S.A, in Britain Frank Bailey, owner of a record shop in unfashionable Southend, began to do the same thing. Essentially, Frank produced a magazine called "Record Mart", which listed rare rockabilly and rock 'n' roll records for sale, using an auction format. Frank was basically a jazz music buff, so he employed Derek Glenister to run the rock 'n' roll side of things.

What Derek did was form a Record label and, using the same format as Weiser, contacted American labels to arrange leases for long forgotten and rare rockabilly recordings. Normally no more than 2000 at a time, just enough to fuel a feeding frenzy amongst collectors. Eventually these re-pressings became valuable, and thus collectable as well. This was replicated in Europe too, especially in Holland and, later, to a lesser extent, France.

And then there were the bootlegs. Suddenly there appeared albums such as 'Elvis live at the Louisiana Hayride', pressed on a reproduced (but deliberately aged) SUN label, although Sam Phillips never recorded Elvis at the Hayride, and there were many others. There were also a few selected dealers who travelled to the U.S. and scoured warehouses full of old vinyl and, once there, would arm themselves with boxes of singles and albums, selling them to specialist record outlets in the UK.

It wasn't beyond some of the more unscrupulous of these dealers to deliberately destroy copies of rare records so that they could justifiably claim that these were very rare copies indeed. With that, up went the price, and thus their profits!

Many rock 'n' roll legends, who had long since forgotten their moment of fame in a studio, were being hunted down by British promoters and labels, such as Charley Records. Some of these 'stars' had moved away from music; Joe Clay, for instance, was found driving a bus and thought that the initial approach inviting him to England to headline a festival was a joke. The name Charlie Feathers was so obscure, with just a few references in archived recording lists, that some didn't even know if he really existed or not! But Charly Records tracked him down and bought him over to England, where he performed at the Rainbow Theatre in north London. Many other performers were enticed over, and had to use prompt sheets and listen to their, by now twenty-year-old, recordings because they had forgotten the tunes and the words!

Meanwhile, disc jockeys like Keith Pinnell known as the fifties Flash, Roy Williams (of Nervous Records), and many more were spinning rock n' roll and rockabilly records at hundreds of small record hops (discos) throughout Great Britain. Britain had the biggest contingent of rock 'n' roll fans thanks to the second generation, Teddy Boys. Small pubs and clubs hosted rock 'n' roll nights, often featuring bands playing original rock 'n' roll, such as The Flying Saucers, Shakin' Stevens and the Sunsets, Vernon and the Gi's, and others.

In the wilds of Wales there emerged a band called Crazy Cavan n' the Rhythm Rockers, who played a stylised form of rockabilly; they had recorded a couple of albums in Holland, and then they hit

London and became an almost instant favourite of the Teddy Boy crowd. A short while later there was also a band called the Tom Cats, who basically couldn't get anyone in the U.S.A. mainstream music industry interested. So the story goes, they went to England, where they had heard about a massive rock 'n' roll revival, and slept rough on the streets (actually it was in an office) whilst touting around for a gig.

Somehow the Tom Cats met performer and producer Dave Edmonds, who was very impressed by the sounds he heard, and dragged them into the studio to hear some more. They were rebranded as The Stray Cats, and Edmonds would go on to produce hit albums and singles for them, even getting them into the UK pop charts, and they became modern rockabilly legends.

Generally, rock 'n' roll was still a very specialised, although an upcoming, genre. It was rarely mentioned in any of the mainstream media (although New Musical Express occasionally ran pieces) and, for all intents and purposes, it had disappeared. But there were a few independent publications that kept the interest going. New Kommotion was one, and it included serious articles on records, performers, and all manner of rock 'n' roll, R&B and rockabilly music.

Other magazines included Now Dig This, Puttin' on the Style, and Cat Talk. They were usually, at least initially, produced by one person, and more often than not on a photocopier, with only a few copies ever produced. But they circulated around the pubs and clubs. In Holland, some people were producing bootlegs of rare recordings. These were almost impossible to obtain from any conventional record store, so to obtain a copy you had to be in the know.

In 1972, Wembley Stadium staged one of the very first concerts at the venue – in fact, it is often said to have been the first ever concert held at the stadium - but a rock concert featuring the bands Status Quo and Yes had been held in 1969. That the London Rock and Roll Show was a smash hit was a total surprise, because no one knew if anyone would even turn up!

But it attracted thousands of fans who came out to see the performers behind the music. And, of course, the fanatics were also there. Originally billed rock 'n' roll era acts The Platters, The Drifters and The Coasters were unable to perform due to work permit issues, so the show was opened instead with sets from the British rock 'n' roll scene; The Houseshakers, Joe Brown, Emile Ford & the Checkmates, Screaming Lord Sutch, Heinz (backed by Wilko Johnson and John Sparks from Dr. Feelgood), and Billy Fury; as well as songs from Jerry Lee Lewis's sister Linda Gail Lewis. Screaming Lord Sutch almost got the show cancelled when he bought a stripper on stage with him! Garage rockers MC5 were not over-popular with the crowd. Little Richard also got booed when he stopped singing rock 'n' roll and jumped on top of his piano, declaring that everyone should never forget that HE was the King of rock 'n' roll! Also booed was a very new Gary Glitter. At least

Roy Wood's new band, Wizzard, only formed a few weeks previously, got into the swing of things and covered some rock 'n' roll tracks!

The highlight of the concert though, were performances by major stars including Bo Diddley, Jerry Lee Lewis, Little Richard, and Bill Haley and His Comets. The concert ended with an extended performance by Chuck Berry, who at the time was enjoying major chart success in Britain and the U.S.A. with his "My Ding-a-Ling", arguably the least rock 'n' roll song he ever produced, a whimsical piece of pop and probably one of the worst! It was obvious that, much like back in the 1950's, there was a burgeoning movement, a feeling that something was changing, contrary to the music media's belief, who maintained that there was no interest in rock 'n' roll.

The aforementioned Charly Records was founded in France in 1974 by Jean-Luc Young, who had been a promoter of teen concerts, and moved to the UK in 1975. Charly was originally known mainly for American originated jazz and other modern oddities, such as the Bollock Brothers. But in the mid-seventies they began their pioneering work on the legendary Sun Records label, and made these recordings readily available, many for the first time. In 1976 they released a Hank Mizell recording, "Jungle Rock", which was recorded in a garage studio in 1958 by Gene Parsons, owner of Eko Records. The guitarist on the recording was Jim Bobo, and it was originally released as being by Bobo. However, the mistake was rectified on a subsequent pressing. Very few original copies ever saw the light of day; however, in 1970, a Dutch bootlegger included it on a compilation LP, and it began to get airplay in the UK's rock 'n' roll clubs. Charly Records reissued it, and it reached number 3 in the UK Singles Chart, and made it to number 1 in Holland! Suddenly, just as twenty years before in America, there was a tidal wave of interest, beginning in the UK. Ace records, too, had begun re-releasing rare and Old R&B records. This was now a fully-fledged rock 'n' roll revival, and it was moving fast.

According to Wikipedia and other sources, the rock 'n' roll revival represented an attempt, in the midst of psychedelia and progressive rock experimentation, to return to the sparse musical values of mid-1950s rock 'n' roll. It is doubtful whether many of the Teddy Boys or rockers thought that deeply about it to come up with that sort of flowery explanation. To them, experimental and progressive rock was simply 'shit', too loud and far too boring. They couldn't understand why anyone would wish to watch a guitarist play a fifteen-minute guitar solo, regardless of how talented they were. All they wanted was good old rock 'n' roll.

At the height of the revival, it seemed that there were clubs everywhere attended by the Teds, rockers, and even hardened biker groups. Britain's most popular newspaper, The Sun, published articles such as "Twenty things you never knew about Teddy Boys", most of it rubbish, that even the Teds themselves didn't know of! Record companies also recognised that ACE and Charley had hit upon an untapped goldmine, and began scouring their vaults for unheard, and often unreleased, gems. For instance, there was tremendous interest in Buddy Holly and his group, The Crickets, with at least four "Greatest Hits" albums being released, pretty much with the same twenty or so songs on them. MCA, owned by EMI, released a series called 'Rare Rockabilly', containing some very rare, red-hot gems, and there were similar releases from CBS, Imperial and Dot amongst others.

There was also interest in the fashions of the 1950's. Of course, the Teddy Boys with their long drape jackets, drainpipe trousers, thick crepe shoes (called 'brothel creepers'), and boot lace ties were everywhere. But some didn't want or didn't fancy this look, and looked at American fashions from the period. They couldn't dress in 'gab'-jackets, (essentially a copy of American work jackets) or pegged trousers, which they had seen in pictures, because at the time, no one was producing or importing them.

But they did wear donkey jackets (borrowed from building sites) and denim jeans with large turn ups, aping the rural working man of the southern states. The girls, rather than follow the likes of Doris Day, were more likely to follow the fashions of pin up girls such as Betty Page. In London, there was Ted's Corner opposite Victoria railways station, producing off the peg versions of the Teddy Boy drapes, often in a variety of colours. But if one was more discerning, and had some money saved up, it was Jack Geech's Tailoring in Harrow that produced something like the real thing. In Kensington market there was a wonderful outlet for vintage and mid-American retro clothing.

But it didn't stop there. Some decorated their houses in 50's style, following pictures in 1950's magazines picked up at the local market. If you could, add a working jukebox, vintage style sofa by G Plan, and maybe even a 1950's style kitchen... small, impractical, but authentic.

The ultimate, of course, would be to get hold of an American car; Chevrolets, Pontiacs, Buicks and Cadillacs began to cruise the streets of the UK, even though the cars were far too big for the small roads and streets. If your budget couldn't run to that, perhaps the British equivalent; Ford's Consul (Mark II) and early Zephyrs, both of whom had some features designed in Detroit, were the favourites.

The 1970's in Britain is remembered by the media and many others as a time for glam rock, and the emergence of performers such as T Rex, Sweet, Mud and the Bay City Rollers; but for many more, it was a huge revival of rock 'n' roll and rockabilly. And yet STILL the BBC refused to acknowledge its existence through its programming, and with good reason. It emerged that the BBC had either discarded, destroyed or simply filmed over many of the original TV programmes that featured original rock 'n' roll and its stars. Realisation dawned upon an unsuspecting world that historical performances by the likes of Cliff Richards, Billy Fury, Tommy Steele, Gene Vincent, Eddie Cochran and others, had all probably been lost, all because the BBC felt that no one would ever be interested in them in the future and film was expensive! Consequently, the BBC very rarely included any rock 'n' roll on its programmes, because they simply didn't have any!

The fanatical rock 'n' roll fans in Britain at the time, organised themselves and marched down London's famous Oxford Street on Saturday May 15th, 1976, accompanied by a couple of bands playing live on the back of flatbed trucks, demanding that the BBC include some rock 'n' roll programming into their regular schedule. The events leading up to this march, and subsequent epic concert, began in the dark winter days of 1975. It started as an idea to gather rock 'n' roll fans from all over the country to join forces to demand more time on radio for original rock 'n' roll. There was some doubt whether the march would ever take place, but after months of planning, publicity, and promotion in the clubs and pubs up and down the country, the day arrived and there outside Hyde Park, London, was the amazing sight of thousands of people, nearly all Teddy Boys and girls resplendent in their best gear, ready to march - and march they did! The event, which saw estimates of up to 20,000 in the capital, (although the actually figure was probably nearer 10,000), finished at Broadcasting House in Wood Lane, White City, London W12, home of the BBC, where a 50.000 strong petition and a taped pilot rock 'n' roll show were handed in. The event culminated at Picketts Lock in north London, where three of the UK's top bands, had been booked to play. The protest was a success, and the BBC caved in. They gave Stuart Coleman a slot and he began to deliver a weekly rock 'n' roll show on Radio 1. He described his show's content as "Blue Suede radio".

At one time in London during the 70's, there were live band appearances on every night of the week somewhere, (seven nights to rock!), and clubs and pubs sprang up in every region of the country. The highlight of the month for many, though, were the visits to The Lyceum Ballroom in the Strand, where bands would play to a large gathering of Teds, bikers, rockers, and some strange folk calling themselves 'rockabillies'. Just as the revival reached its peak, a new music craze hit London, and later the country, called Punk Rock, led by the iconic and self-styled anti-social, group, The Sex Pistols. They were followed by youngsters with hair dyed in all colours of the rainbow, sported safety pins and chains through their ears, noses and elsewhere, indulged in drugs, and wore bondage and fetish clothing, often shredded to pieces. The Teddy Boys and rockers united against what they saw as an enemy, an enemy that would undermine the morals of Britain's youth (sound familiar?).

The upshot of this were pitched battles along London's fashionable Kings Road, with hundreds from both sides beating hell out of each other on a weekly basis.

On the rock 'n' roll scene, just like during the 1950's, there were entrepreneurs who would jump on the bandwagon. They would organise events, often operating on the same night as another event, just streets apart. Promoters began arguing with each other, claiming territorial rights, and basically splitting the scene. Fans didn't know whether to go to one club or a variety of clubs, and bands didn't care - they'd go wherever they were paid! There were also tensions between the Teds and the new rockabillies. The Teds claimed ownership of rock 'n' roll, and dismissed rockabilly as jumped-up country music; which, in some ways, it was. The Teds claimed that they and rock 'n' roll were on the scene first, conveniently ignoring that fact that when the Teds/Edwardians first emerged, rock 'n' roll music hadn't! It was all becoming too much, and it seemed almost overnight, at the end of the 70's, that the whole scene imploded; clubs cancelled, and rock 'n' roll and rockabilly fell out of fashion. And that was that. The media circus moved on. The scene grew back of course, but it was slow. And it wasn't the same. There were reduced clubs, and the rock 'n' roll and rockabilly fanatics were left to themselves - a good thing in many people's eyes. But by the mid to late 1980's, the scene in the UK had reached the same intensity as it had during the revival, and it would continue to grow into the new millennium and beyond.

CHAPTER SEVEN

And thus, up to date

Even by the time the revival had collapsed in the UK and Europe, America still hadn't quite got a grip on what was going on. It took an Englishman to show them what it was all about, and what they had been missing. Tom Ingram was well known as a rockabilly DJ and promoter in the UK, where he performed at, and later ran, London's top rockabilly clubs. He also presented rockabilly radio shows for stations that included BBC Radio One, and later for independent radio stations that broadcast to countries across the world. He founded the world famous Hemsby Rock n' Roll weekenders, and brought fellow promoter, Willie Jeffrey, on board. One of the ideas that they were arranging, was to organise a similar weekend in the US, and Tom had gone to America with a view to discovering whether that was feasible. However, following an acrimonious disagreement, Tom and Willie parted company, and Tom, began to concentrate on the U.S.A. His idea was to find a suitable location, so he came up with and organised the Viva Las Vegas rockabilly weekender, with the help of Barney Koumis of No Hit Records. Originally set in The Gold Coast Hotel & Casino in 1998, it became an almost instant hit, to the point where it outgrew the hotel, and in 2009 relocated to The Orleans Hotel & Casino. It is now known as the Viva Las Vegas Rockabilly Weekend, an annual 4-day music festival and car show that takes place every Easter weekend. VLV has grown to be the largest event of its type in the world. It features bands and fans from all over the globe, and includes a large Classic Car Show. Tom works hard on promoting the event, but also in educating America, often appearing on chat shows and conducting interviews where he explains what rockabilly music is, and where it came from.

The fact that he has to, is an indication that, whilst there is at least some awareness of rockabilly and real rock 'n' roll in the USA, both are seen as something akin to a carnival novelty act. Something that happens maybe once a year, and is much like a fancy-dress party. Their thoughts are that one hires or makes some sort of costume for the event. They were, and still often are, completely taken aback when they come across these people, staring at them as though they had just landed from Mars! They are astonished when they discover that these folks, who have travelled from all corners of the globe, actually dress like this all the time, don't like the Beatles, (almost sacrilege in the US), drive 1950's cars, and live their lives totally immersed in a retro lifestyle!

By the same token, many European fans travel to the USA and are disappointed to find that places they had perhaps only heard about, maybe in a song, were not stuck in a 1950's time warp! Many visitors to Lubbock, Texas, found that the city, until relatively recently, had never heard of Buddy Holly, let alone erected any sort of memorial to its most famous son. Nowadays in Lubbock there is almost an overload, with numerous streets, shopping malls and other attractions bearing a Buddy Holly connection. The only other city attraction is the museum celebrating the history of the western saddle!

Memphis visitors almost invariably end up at Graceland, Elvis Presley's celebrated home, to find that the small white mansion is indeed smaller than they imagined, but just as interesting anyway. However, the shopping parade opposite is full of retail outlets selling nasty, often tacky, and quite expensive souvenirs. If one visits Memphis, then a preferred tourist attraction ought to be the SUN Studios at Union Avenue, and Beale Street, where Elvis would visit to listen to the various Blues musicians.

Rockabilly and rock 'n' roll today have changed beyond all recognition to what it was, even in the aftermath of the rock 'n' roll revival in the 1970's. For instance, during the 1970's and well into the 1980's, many of the original performers, regardless of age or talent remaining, were lured to the UK and Europe to headline at festivals. They might have gone into a studio, perhaps for as little as a day in the 1950's, and cut one or two original tunes that either were or were not released, and almost certainly didn't sell in enough numbers to dent the charts. These artists then drifted back to their lives. They were not as clued up in those

days, and there are cases where some original performers were unaware that their recordings had,
in fact, been pressed to vinyl at all, and although
these records might not have sold thousands, one
would have thought the performer might have
been due SOME royalties, even if it only amounted
to a handful of dollars! Very often, because they
had only one song, they would struggle to put any
sort of set together, therefore would resort to covering standard rockabilly and rock 'n' roll songs.
This happened so often that it became almost a
standard format...performing covers and culmi-
nating their act with their one and only 'hit' (sic),
performed at the end of a set which had included
such standards as "Good Rockin' Tonight", "Whole
Lotta Shakin' Going on", "Blue Moon of Kentucky",
the ubiquitous "Blue Suede Shoes", and others.
This was all lapped up by the audiences. For the
performers it was a total culture shock, as well as
being a pleasant, if unexpected, bonus payday.
That anyone had remembered their one moment
of fame was a huge surprise, but then to face an
army of guys and girls who often knew the lyrics
better than they did themselves, was astonishing to them. When faced with these people, who
looked as though they had just stepped out of the
"American Graffiti" film set, it is little wonder that
the performers sometimes froze, facing the biggest
audience of their lives, often looking like the pro-
verbial rabbit caught in the headlights!

This was all well and good, but it simply couldn't
continue. In 1977, Elvis Presley, the man who had
opened the door, passed away. It was no surprise

that there was a universal outpouring of grief from the fans. But from a performers point of view, there was almost a collective slump. Would anyone still want to see them now that the King had gone? Well, yes, they would; the 1980's and 1990's still saw large festivals in the UK, normally headlined by an original artist, often labelled as a 'legendary performer'. Knowledgeable audiences were beginning to see through them though. Many of the performers were a long way past their sell by date, and audiences were getting fed up with the, by now tired, format. Slowly but surely, they were passing away. Festival organisers became more desperate, finding and hiring more obscure original artists. And, of course, they inspired a lot of wannabe musicians to try it themselves. Thus, slowly, they have been replaced by thousands of newer and much younger artists and bands, the members of whom are far more savvy than their 50's counterparts, and with access to far more sophisticated equipment. They write their own material, quite rare in the 1950's, and get it recorded themselves, often using modern, easily available and affordable technology. They play at a myriad of clubs and festivals. A select few, such as Darrel Higham (from the UK), Jack Baymoore, Eva Eastwood, the Go Getters, (all from Sweden), Big Sandy, (from the USA), Phil Haley and the Comments (guess who they sound like?!), John Lewis, The Houserockers and a few others are actually really really good, but again, far more sophisticated and knowledgeable than their original counterparts. As for the majority of the rest, the music has its roots in rockabilly and rock 'n' roll, and their stage attire often looks authentic; like the audiences, they dress and pander to a stylised 'American dream' of mid-50s America that may or may not have ever really existed. But generally, the music isn't the same as it was. Rockabilly music, originally, was always a dangerous beast.

Darrel Hugham

It had come about as a hybrid, borrowing heavily from the Blues and R&B, Hillbilly, Country and Western, and, to a lesser extent, from the crazes such as boogie woogie, sometimes with even a little Cajun influence. All of these styles were at some time borrowed, merged if you like, moulded together to create a totally unique sound. It was raw, edgy and exciting. But it only lasted for about four years in its purest form, from about 1954 to

1958, and even during that time, perceptibly moving on to what was eventually termed rock 'n' roll, where saxophones, horns and pianos were incorporated into the sound. Rock 'n' roll itself moved away from its purest sound in 1956 and 1957, and by 1958, the industry and the establishment had begun its sustained attack on this 'jungle music'; it became a parody of itself, with performers delivering a syrupy version, still termed as rock 'n' roll, but not nearly as potent. That 'pop' sound also evolved, the black version into soul, and the white version into what was labelled 'beat', and later on rock. Today's version of rockabilly and rock 'n' roll is far more street wise, and the variety of sounds and styles is mind blowing. However, in comparison, a lot of the bands are often quite bland, and generally lack the edge of the original. To be honest, some of these bands wouldn't be out of place at your average wedding reception!

Anyone asking to hear a typical rockabilly piece is nearly always prompted to listen to one of the originals, rather than what it has evolved into. And yet, the fact remains that the basic structures of rockabilly and rock 'n' roll music remain the same. It is inconceivable to hear a rockabilly song containing lyrics that applaud the virtues of free living, love and peace. I have never heard a rockabilly record that contains gratuitous bad language, or is calling the gangs to take drugs or fight on the streets. Perhaps the tongue in cheek, "Rumble in Brighton Tonight" by The Stray Cats might go into the last category, but generally the structure has remained the same. And therein lies the problem. Relevance.

It is no longer relevant to modern youngsters, thus of little interest to them. In Britain, the largest group of rock 'n' roll fans, the Teddy Boys, or Teds, had evolved into a parody of themselves. With all the glitz and showmanship that seemed to go hand in hand with what is known as the glam rock era, the original Edwardians had begun to disappear as the new generation of Teds, with their brightly coloured drapes, took over. There was trouble with the punk rockers, there was internal trouble with the rockabillies, but most of all, there was the onslaught from new music styles that took over the high street and the broadcast media. The Teds retreated to back street pubs and clubs to enjoy the music on their own terms. This was as a result of the collapse of the scene. As we have said, by the 1980's the scene, such as it was, began to recover, but without the glamour and media attention of the 70's. It did recover, but in odd ways. Suddenly there seemed to be an influx of rock 'n' roll fans that tried to dress the part. Many of them seemed to have taken their clothing styles from 'Grease' and 'Happy Days'. They would turn up at club events and jive the night away, even though the hardcore looked down on them and labelled them as 'jive bunnies', or 'plastic' rock 'n' rollers. Many rock n' roll and rockabilly events took on the atmosphere of a sort of birthday or fancy dress party. They were of no harm to anyone, but at least they kept the clubs going.

The problem is, though, these people and the 70's Teds are now middle aged, and there is less and less new young blood coming into and becoming interested in the scene, and the ones that are already in it are not particularly encouraged to entice others to join in. It is a difficult problem to overcome. Rockabilly and rock 'n' roll are defined by what they originally were, and most of those who play, love and listen to the music would not have it any other way. Of course, some have tried to write more sophisticated lyrics, and even to modernise the music, but without much success. Some groups have even tried to perform covers of 1980's pop songs, such as "Tainted love" and others, in a rockabilly style, but to be honest, it rarely works. Rockabilly and rock 'n' roll, by their very nature, are strictly defined by the original structure, and if one tries to move away from that, then it's no longer acceptable to a traditional rockabilly or rock 'n' roll audience.

The last man standing, Jerry Lee Lewis, passed away in 2022, and just to accentuate the fact, the lesser known, but equally as talented, Charlie Gracie and Johnny Powers both followed a couple of weeks later. There are no more original American performers of note left. It sometimes feels as though this fantastic rock 'n' roll coaster ride is finally coming to an end.

Everyone appreciates that the music has lasted far longer than anyone imagined or predicted. The "flash in the pan" is still with us and loved across the world. But, without a new generation of people coming onto and buying into the scene, the music will be played less and less. As immediate popularity wanes, fewer people will be attending the festivals and the clubs, and as the promoters feel the pinch, they will begin to close. Many don't attend their local rock n' roll clubs any more, preferring to go to one or two of the big festivals. I cannot say that clubs will die out en masse, as there will always be one or two that keep the club scene going, but they would probably operate at a loss. But, unless something changes dramatically, it is entirely conceivable that within the next twenty years or so, the rock 'n' roll/rockabilly scene could simply cease to exist, killed by a lack of participants and interest.

Perhaps the problem is overkill. I have often witnessed groups of modern youngsters travelling to London to see a live performance from their favourite pop or rock band. They are excited, not only about seeing their heroes in the flesh, but actually hearing them play live as well! And yet, in the UK the rockabilly/rock 'n' roll scene features live bands EVERY week. To see a live band at least once a week, sometimes more, is not an unusual occurrence. And, because of that, audiences become a little blasé and far more critical. Far too often, bands turn up at a local club and run through their routines without any semblance of stage presence or structure to the show that they put on, and certainly without any of the impact that would make them stand out as their predecessors did. Rockabilly and rock 'n' roll stood out in the 1950's because it was different, it was new, raw, and very exciting, and because of that, to a certain extent, they didn't need to be showmen, because of the controversy surrounding their music.

Nowadays, bands set up their gear and blandly run

through their set, often applauded and cheered on by their audiences, more often than not more wildly and enthusiastically after a good few alcoholic drinks have been consumed. But, just as often, members of those audiences will return home to their social media sites and let the world know via the internet, that the band were not all they were cracked up to be. Whilst the worldwide rockabilly/rock 'n' roll scene is widespread, it is very parochial, and word, especially on the internet, gets around quickly. The other factors are somewhat out of their control. Rising and exorbitant travelling costs mean that very often bands won't travel too far away from their natural homes. Even those that agree to play at some of the large festivals, do so, certainly not for a big fee and not so much for the pleasure of playing in front of a big audience, but for the kudos an appearance at a well-regarded festival potentially brings. At some of the big events, there are representatives of the independent record labels and studios that specialise in rockabilly and rock 'n' roll. The bands all hope for an introduction to these labels, dreaming of getting an album recorded and put together.

But modern life also brings different problems. There are so many different types of music and activities that youngsters can do with their leisure time; although a few get into rock 'n' roll and rockabilly, many more are just as happy sitting at home playing on their Play-stations, X Boxes or, if they do go out, attending venues that play the sort of music the commercial radio stations hypnotically pump out 24 hours a day, 7 days a week, 365 days a year. Even after that great march in the 1970's, the BBC and other mainstream commercial stations still don't broadcast a definitive 'go to' programme on a regular basis. Those wanting to hear the music from home or at work have to connect via the internet and find specialised stations.

As I mentioned, there ARE some top performers out there, from various parts of the world, which is great, but they mostly turn up at the big festivals. It is an unfortunate, but very true, fact that a large percentage of bands aspiring to play rockabilly or rock 'n' roll are distinctly average pub bands, and some of them, frankly, are awful. There are festivals where the audience figures are good...Viva Las Vegas, for instance, attracts around 20,000 over four or five days from all over the world, whilst festivals in the UK get between 3,000 and 8,000, depending on the venue; but the audiences are treated poorly. They are expected, especially in the UK, to cram into very badly maintained holiday camps in the off season, that are often a disgrace, and which your average holiday maker wouldn't endure. Why do people keep attending? There is a strong argument that suggests that many of them attend for the social aspect, to meet up with old friends and people they'd met the year before, or had chatted with on social media. The music is, in some cases, dare I say it, almost incidental.

On the other side of the coin, there are clubs that run every week throughout the year and they don't enjoy such audiences. A good audience at a rockabilly or rock 'n' roll club in the UK tends to number between 60 and 100. Sometimes, for a particularly good performer, numbers may reach around 150. This is not, by modern event standards, a good turnout. You'd think that rockabilly and rock 'n' roll fans would turn out in their numbers for one of the top bands, but this isn't a rule that can be relied on.

Because there is so much available, audiences will go where their mates go, and when that happens, somebody will lose out. One might have thought that the scene, in the UK especially, might have learned the lesson from the collapse at the end of the 1970's. Apparently not, as there are so many competing events going on, that it is often difficult to choose which one to attend! I am aware that some attend almost every event staged. Quite how, I am not sure, as these events can turn out to be very expensive; some spend as much in a weekend as other people might spend on a week's holiday!

However, if the music is to survive, things need to change. And to make those changes, promoters, musicians, specialist radio stations, the rockabilly/rock 'n' roll media, and, yes, the bands too, would actually have to get together, literally, and try to work out what can be done. This would require talking to each other seriously and sensibly, sadly not something that happens very often, and then bringing forward realistic workable ways to keep the music and the scene alive. This would probably involve an enormous promotional and marketing exercise on a monumental scale that has never been seen before. Incidentally, Tom Ingram, before moving to America, did actually organise a meeting of like-minded promoters; although, as he states, whilst the meeting was 'productive', because he was in the process of shifting his operations across the Atlantic, nothing ever came of it. An opportunity missed then.

Why is it important that rockabilly and rock 'n' roll is kept alive in the first place? Rockabilly and rock 'n' roll, when presented and played well, has the ability to impact on audiences. It is the sort of impact they talk about for weeks afterwards, and makes one feel like it's something that one has just discovered. Rockabilly, rock 'n' roll and original R&B are, quite simply, the roots of all modern 'pop' music, and that should not be ignored by the modern world. When it is played well, it is by far the most exciting. But not only that, rock 'n' roll, and to a lesser extent rockabilly, was, to use a modern idiom, a game changer. It literally did help to change society and attitudes. It is quite shocking that only half a century ago, a black person could not stay in the same hotel, could not share the same stage or even get on a bus, without being segregated or abused, both verbally and, occasionally, physically. If it never did anything else, rock 'n' roll was instrumental (still no pun intended) in enabling changes to be made, changes in our way of thinking, and our social attitudes. Of course, as the world began to modernise, segregation, slavery, abuse and much else, ended. Such changes never happen unless a majority of people, the people that a social change like this actually affects, recognise that it's a good idea and are happy with it. Rock 'n' roll helped significantly to break down barriers and make a contribution to bringing black and white people together.

They say that history makes us what we are, and the thought that this music, representing our very recent history, could be dismissed as insignificant, could simply fade away, ignored by a modern world which spends most of its leisure time on the internet and social media, is simply unacceptable.

As a Teddy Boy once said, "it is better to listen to bad rock 'n' roll, than none at all!"

CHAPTER EIGHT

Author's note: I am fairly sure that if asked, most rocka-billy and rock n' roll fans would be able to produce lists of their favourite performers. There would be arguments as to who should be included and excluded. The following is a list of performers that influenced me and should not be read as any sort of definitive list.

Selected R&B Performers

Cab Calloway

Cab, born as Cabell Calloway III, was an American singer, songwriter, bandleader, conductor and dancer. He is perhaps more associated with Jazz – swing, and was noted for his flamboyant dress sense and stage antics. But his music was essentially different to other jazz performers at the time, and nowadays is firmly recognised as one of the pioneers of R&B music. He was a regular performer at the Cotton Club in Harlem. He was a master of scat singing, and had several hit records; "Minnie the Moocher", was the first single to reach over a million in sales, and he later appeared in films, including 'The Cincinnati Kid' (1965), and 'Hello Dolly!' And 'The Blues Brothers'.

Tiny Bradshaw

was an American jazz and rhythm and blues

bandleader, singer, composer, pianist, and drummer. His biggest hit was "Well Oh Well" in 1950, and the following year he recorded "The Train Kept A-Rollin'", important to the development of rock and roll; he co-wrote and sang on both records.

He formed his first band in 1934, adopting a style similar to that of Cab Calloway, and he concentrated on novelty tunes such as "The Sheik of Araby", "the Dark Town Strutter's Ball" and "The Jersey Bounce". For the duration of World War II, Tiny and his orchestra toured the world, entertaining troops. Upon demobilization, he found that large orchestras were no longer economic, so reduced his band to a nine piece, and later a seven-piece band. Buddy Holly was later to cite Tiny as a formative influence on his career.

Hank Ballard & The Midnighters

The underrated Hank Ballard first came to prominence as a member of the Royals, where his high pitch tenor voice, somewhat akin to Clyde McPlatter's, helped to promote "Git it", into the R&B top ten. This, and the fact that the song was very risqué, a common factor within R&B at the time, saw The Royals hit the Top Ten for the first time. There were various arguments within R&B, some saying that the music was simply smut, whilst others pointed out that this was exactly what R&B was all about, to be edgy and suggestive. Ballard certainly took the latter view, and his next song was called, "Sock it to me Mary". But the song was so risqué that Ralph Bass, the group's producer, asked Ballard to rewrite it. Hank's wife, Annie, was pregnant at the time, and Ballard changed the lyrics and the title to "Work with me Annie". The song was uniformly banned across the nation's radio stations, but still sold well enough to inspire a deluge of answer records!

It was around this time that the name of the group was changed to The Midnighters, and they should be remembered for some of the best R&B ever made, including titles such as, "Sexy Ways", "Open up the Back Door" and "Baby Please". But if the Midnighters, and indeed Hank Ballard, are to be remembered for just one song, it has to be the one that made a million worldwide, but not for him. Hank and the Midnighters had released a song called "Teardrops on Your Letter", which on the B side had "The Twist". The disk's progress was slow, based on the A Side, but another performer, Ernest Evans, better known as Chubby Checker, asked to record the B side, and with the help of some useful promotion from Bandstand's Dick Clark, the song shot to the top of the charts across the world. Hank Ballard's own version was re-released to try and cash in, and reached number 28 in the charts. But it could have been so much more.

"Big" Joe Turner

If one had to pick out an absolute superstar from R&B, then Joe Turner would have to be a contender for the title. Joe Turner was known as a blues 'shouter', although he was steeped in the world of jazz. Together with Pianist Pete Johnson, Joe played Kansas City's clubs and speakeasys during the prohibition period. So popular were they, that they also ventured out to Chicago and St Louis, and continued to do so until 1936, even though prohibition ended in 1933! At one such event they ran into John Hammond, an A & R (artists & repertoire) man for Colombia Records, and he invited them to perform at the first "Spirituals of Swing" concert in 1938. Their performance was so impressive that they were invited to/began to record for the Vocalian label, who released such titles as "Roll 'em Pete" and "Going Away Blues". Following a brief return to Kansas City, Joe and Pete ventured back to New York, playing many of the city's most prestigious venues, including the Harlem Apollo, often guesting with other big name blues and jazz ensembles.

In 1951, Ahmet Ertegun and Herb Abramson. who founded the Atlantic label in 1947, signed Big Joe to their roster. Joe's first recording for the label, "Chains of Love", was a huge hit that spent more than six months on the R&B chart. This monster success was followed by more titles such as "Sweet Sixteen", "Honey Hush" and "TV Mama", establishing Joe as the number one performer in R&B.

With the advent of rock 'n' roll, Ahmet Ertegun decided to re-model Joe to appeal to the rock 'n' roll crowd. Thus were recorded, "Shake, Rattle 'n' Roll", "Flip, Flop 'n' Fly", "Lipstick Powder and Paint", and many more that cemented Joe into the annals of rock 'n' roll history.

Towards the end of his life, the portly, swaggering Joe, with Pete Johnson in tow, moved down to New Orleans and, even after Pete passed away in 1967, Joe kept performing until he too shed his mortal coil, suffering from kidney failure in 1985.

Jackie Brenston

There is only one piece of music by which Jackie Brenston is remembered, and even that was an outright copy of another song. "Rocket 88", often cited as the first ever rock 'n' roll record, was recorded at Sam Phillips Sun studio, and released by Leonard Chess on his new Chess label. However, it emerged that the song was exactly the same as Jimmie Liggin's "Cadillac Boogie", although rearranged. When asked, Brenston candidly admitted the fact, and that all he had done was substitute the cars involved! Other than that, Jackie Brenston's career was a stop-start affair, mainly due to the fact that his preferred hobby was drinking, a pursuit which he practised enthusiastically and to excess, probably at the cost of a promising career as a performer.

Sister Rosetta Tharpe

She began her career singing gospel, and at age six, Tharpe had joined her mother as a regular performer in a travelling evangelical troupe. Billed as a "singing and guitar playing miracle," she accompanied her mother in performances that were part sermon and part gospel concert before audiences across the American South. In the mid-1920s, Tharpe and her mother settled in Chicago, Illinois, where they performed religious concerts at the Roberts Temple on 40th Street, occasionally travelling to perform at church conventions throughout the country. Tharpe developed considerable fame as a musical prodigy, standing out in an era when prominent black female guitarists were rare. In 1934, aged 19, she married Thomas Thorpe, a preacher, who accompanied her and her mother on many of their tours. The marriage lasted only a few years, after her husband physically abused her, but she decided to adopt a version of her husband's surname as her stage name, Sister Rosetta Tharpe.

In 1938, she left her husband and moved with her mother to New York City. Soon afterwards, she began a relationship, both on and off stage, with Marie Knight, a gospel singer. At a time when homosexual and lesbian relationships were outlawed, it was a brave venture. She then joined Cab Calloway's Band, but there was a conflict of interest, certainly in Calloway's view, as she would often perform other concerts with Maria Knight. She left in 1940 and joined Lucky Millander's Band.

Sister Rosetta Tharpe is remembered as having an uninhibited electric guitar style, she was a pioneer in her guitar technique; and was among the first popular recording artists to use heavy distortion on her electric guitar, opening the way to the rise of electric blues. Her guitar-playing technique predated rock 'n' roll guitar playing in the 1950's, and had a profound influence on many musicians including Chuck Berry, Ronnie Wood, and indeed the development of British blues in the 1960s.

Selected Rockabilly Performers

Carl Perkins

Carl Perkins' songs personified the rockabilly era, and Carl Perkins' sound personifies the rockabilly sound more so than anybody involved in it, because he never changed. Carl and his band arrived and auditioned for Sam Phillips at Sun Records around the time that Elvis was about to join RCA, so found that Phillips was looking for a new 'big' act. It was fate that decided Carl wasn't going to be the one. Carl wrote and recorded "Blue Suede Shoes", which was released on January 1, 1956, and became a massive chart success. In the United States, it reached number 1 on Billboard magazine's country music chart (the only number 1 success he would have) and number 2 on the Billboard Best Sellers popular music chart.

On March 22nd, Carl and his band were on the way to New York to appear on NBC-TV's Perry Como Show. "Blue Suede Shoes" had sold more than

500,000 copies by March 22nd, and Sam Philips had planned to celebrate by presenting Perkins with a gold record on The Perry Como Show. Shortly before sunrise , on Route 13 between Dover and Woodside, Delaware, their vehicle hit the back of a pickup truck and went into a ditch containing about 12 inches of water. Drummer DS Holland had to pull Perkins, unconscious, from the water. Perkins had sustained three fractured vertebrae in his neck, a severe concussion, a broken collar bone, and lacerations all over his body. Perkins remained unconscious for an entire day. What the crash also did, was ensure that Perkins was out of action for just over a year but, despite some limited success, he never reached his potential in the way that Elvis did. Carl Perkins is often referred to as the 'The Father of Rockabilly'.

The Rock and Roll Trio

Mention the name of Johnny Burnette, and most people might think of Johnny the pop star with his hits such as "Dreamin' " and "You're Sixteen". However, to most rockabilly fans, Johnny was, together with his brother Dorsey and guitarist Paul Birlison, a member of the hottest rockabilly band around.

Johnny, Dorsey and Paul all met when they were young boxers, and all three won Golden Gloves boxing awards in their home town of Memphis. They formed a group and began performing locally, mixing country music and blues into a style that is now described as 'rockabilly'. Being in Memphis, they were aware of Elvis, but there is some debate as to whether the Trio ever recorded at Sun. The trio were said to have auditioned, but were turned down by Sam Phillips, apparently because they sounded too much like Elvis! Whether or not this audition took place, however, remains a matter of dispute. Dorsey Burnette has stated that they recorded a demo session for Sun. He said, "We took Sam Phillips some songs and he turned 'em down, but they weren't very good anyway." In an article for TV Radio Mirror, Johnny Burnette recalled that he and Dorsey had auditioned for Sun Records, although no tapes of any such audition have ever been found; but this could be explained by the fact that Sam Phillips was prone to record over tapes. More importantly, however, Burlison later insisted that the group did not audition at Sun at all.

By 1956, the trio had built a strong reputation in and around Memphis. But the earnings from these sessions did not provide them with enough to live on. In February/March 1956, they decided to drive to New York city. When they arrived in the city, they found out about the Wednesday night auditions for the Ted Mack Original Amateur Hour, and they joined the endless queue of show business hopefuls. They won three straight appearances in April and May 1956, which gained them a slot on the finalists' tour on 9 September 1956 - their appearance, unfortunately, being telecast live from New York on the same night as Elvis Presley's first appearance on the Ed Sullivan Show, which was also beamed live, from Los Angeles, and captured the highest viewing share in the history of US television. A newspaper clip on the day after their third win on the Ted Mack Show referred to them as "the Rock and Roll Boys from Memphis".Following this, they signed to Coral Records and, along with session musicians Buddy Harmon on drums and renowned guitarist, Grady Martin, proceeded to cut some of the hottest rockabilly ever made, but sadly none of it made the national charts.

Venues began billing the group as Johnny Burnette and the Rock and Roll Trio on live dates. This name was used on their first two singles, and on their third single they were known as The Johnny Burnette Trio. Dorsey was incensed by this, as he had taken the lead on a few songs, including "Sweet Love on My Mind", "My Love You're A Stranger" and "Blues Stay Away From Me". He wanted to retain the more democratic name Rock and Roll Trio, despite the fact that the group was now a quartet.

The band was constantly on the road, completing what seemed to be an endless stream of one-night stands in order to cover their living expenses. This exhausting regime led to squabbles, which were exacerbated by lack of chart success. These squabbles finally came to a head at a gig in Niagara Falls in the fall of 1956, where, after a fight, Dorsey quit the group. In 1957, Coral released a 10" LP, which was entitled "Johnny Burnette and the Rock 'n Roll Trio" (Coral CRL 57080). It did not include their first single "Tear It Up", but that was later added to a reissued version of the album. For anyone not familiar with rockabilly music, the music that the trio made is nearly always cited as a good place to start, such is their legacy.

Charlie Feathers

He started out as a session musician at Sun Studios, playing any side instrument he could in the hopes of someday making his own music there. It was rumoured that Sam Phillips didn't think much of him, and even had him sweeping the studios occasionally! Never a shy man, he eventually got his chance, playing on a small label started by Sam Phillips called Flip Records, which got him enough attention to record a couple of singles for both Sun and Holiday Inn Records. Feathers also made the audacious claim that he had arranged "That's All Right" and "Blue Moon of Kentucky" for Elvis Presley, and later claimed that his "We're Getting Closer (To Being Apart)" had been intended to be Elvis' sixth single for Sun. He did eventually get a bone fide record on Sun, "I Forgot To Remember To Forget", when the writer Stan Kesler asked him to record a demo of the song.

When it became clear that he was not part of Sam Phillip's plans, he moved on to Meteor Records, and then King Records, where he recorded his best-known work. His 1950s singles included "Peepin' Eyes", "Defrost Your Heart", "Tongue-Tied Jill" and "Bottle to the Baby". When his King contract ran out, he still claimed that he thought there was a conspiracy to keep his music from gaining the popularity it deserved, although quite where the logic behind this came from was unclear.

When the rock n roll revival started in the UK in the 1970's, Feathers was tracked down and booked to appear, and was a great success, even though he claimed that he "taught Elvis everything I know", and that he was the originator of the rockabilly sound. He passed away in 1998, but his music remains popular with many rockabilly fans.

Roy Hall

His real name was James Faye Hall, but he adopted the name Roy following the death of one of the members of the band he was playing in. He was also sometimes known as Sunny David, although this may have been so that he could record for another label without infringing any copyright issues, a common practice in the 1940s. He formed his own five-piece band, the Cohutta Mountain Boys, signed for independent record label Fortune Records, in Detroit, Michigan, and in 1949 they cut their first record, a hillbilly boogie-woogie song called "Dirty Boogie". The single became a jukebox favourite in the Midwest; however, its follow-ups, which delved more into traditional country music, failed to match the initial success.

The Cohutta Mountain Boys' popularity earned them, briefly, a supporting role for singer Tennessee Ernie Ford in Nashville. Afterwards, the band continued a journeymen existence, eventually returning to Detroit where Hall assembled a new group, the Eagles, and recorded material for Citation Records.

However, in 1950 Hall moved to Nashville to record two solo singles, both commercially unsuccessful. He then opened a music and gambling club called the Music Box, later renamed the Musicians' Hideaway, where he was a regular performer. Hall claimed that Elvis Presley performed there one night in 1954, but Hall fired him because "he weren't no damn good." He also claimed that, in the same year, Jerry Lee Lewis played there for several weeks.

Roy's biggest claim to fame is that he was the co-writer of the classic "Whole Lotta Shakin' Goin' On", a song recorded by Hall himself, and more famously by Jerry Lee Lewis. Although his writing claim was initially disputed, later reissues of the song credit Hall for his role in its conception. In a recording session for Hall at Decca Records on September 15, 1955, he recorded three songs, including "Whole Lotta Shakin' Goin' On". By this time Big Maybelle had already recorded her own variation of the song, which resulted in a moderate national hit.

Hall's recording contract with Decca concluded in 1956 with no sizeable hit - a consequence of ineffective promoting. Jerry Lee Lewis achieved a number 3 hit in 1957 with "Whole Lotta Shakin' Goin' On", instantly launching him into national prominence. Although Hall was in line for royalties, he didn't get any, and his ex-wife successfully sued for his share. Hall is not credited on early issues of Lewis' single.

Whilst he may not be on many lists of favourite rockabilly performers, Roy's contribution of "Whole Lotta Shakin'..." warrants inclusion, but he also has other songs that are worth listening to, including "Dirty Boogie", a cover version of "Blue Suede Shoes", "Dig that Boogie", and "Rock 'n' Roll Grandpa".

Roy Orbison

Some might find the inclusion of Roy Orbison here a surprise. But Orbison began singing in a rockabilly and country-and-western band as a teenager, and was signed by Sam Phillips in 1956. Whilst he didn't enjoy huge success at Sun, he certainly left an impression, and a song, "Ooby Dooby", which broke into the Billboard Hot 100, peaking at number 59, and selling 200,000 copies.

It has become a standard for rockabilly bands. Much influenced by Elvis Presley, Orbison performed frenetically, doing "..everything we could to get applause because we had only one hit record..".

Orbison also began writing songs in a rockabilly style, including "Go! Go! Go!" and "Rockhouse". Many music historians recognise that Orbison's voice was unique, and arguably the best of any rock singer; they also note that his vocal tones weren't suited to rockabilly. But he gave it a go anyway. He enjoyed his greatest success with Monument Records, recording memorable and heart wrenching ballads, a reflection of his personal life; he lost two sons when his house burnt down whilst he was on tour. Towards the end of his life, he was part of the supergroup, the Traveling Wilburys, along with Bob Dylan, George Harrison, Jeff Lynne and Tom Petty.

Wanda Jackson

Wanda Jackson emerged onto the scene when it was not 'the done thing' for a young female performer to perform on her own; thus she was often chaperoned to live performances by her Father.

She was then discovered by country singer Hank Thompson, who helped her secure a recording contract with Decca Records in 1954. At Decca, Jackson had her first hit single with the country song, "You Can't Have My Love". She then began touring the following year with Elvis Presley. The two briefly dated, and Presley encouraged her to record in the rockabilly style. In 1956, Jackson signed with Capitol Records, where she was given free licence to record both country and rockabilly.

The label released a string of Jackson's rockabilly singles, including "Fujiyama Mama", "Mean Mean Man", and a top 40 hit "Let's Have a Party". The tunes mentioned are just the tip of the Wanda Jackson iceberg, and there is a wealth of others that have gained her acclaimed recognition amongst rockabilly fans.

Johnny Powers

Born John Leon Joseph Pavlik, a guitar player, singer, writer and producer specializing in rockabilly, Powers was best known for his 1957 recording on the now-defunct Fox Records label entitled "Long Blond Hair". Powers began his professional career in 1953 at age 15, when he joined a local Detroit country band known as Jimmy Williams and the Drifters. Later, having become a fan of Carl Perkins and the young Elvis Presley, Powers began to include rock 'n' roll elements in his music. Until 1955, Powers performed and recorded under his birth name but, following a studio session for Fortune Records in Detroit, co-owner Devora Brown – seeing Pavlik eating a PowerHouse candy bar – gave him the stage name of Johnny Powers.

Powers released a pair of singles on the Fox Records label (not to be confused with today's 20th Century Fox Records), including "Long Blond Hair". Fox went out of business soon thereafter, and in 1959 Powers signed with Sun Records, which released one single under his name. In 1960, Powers met with Berry Gordy and signed on with Motown Records, becoming the first white male musician to do so; he is also thought to be the only recording artist to have ever been under contract to both Sun and Motown Records. In his five-year relationship with Motown, Powers devoted most of his energies to producing and writing, rather than recording. Powers died in Michigan on January 16, 2023, at the age of 84.

Janis Martin

Known as the 'The female Elvis', Janis Martin joined RCA just two months after Elvis Presley joined the label. She recorded "Will You Willyum" on March 8, 1956, backed by her own composition "Drugstore Rock 'n Roll". The song became the biggest hit of her career, selling 750,000 records. Soon, Martin was performing on American Bandstand, The Today Show and Tonight Starring Steve Allen. She also appeared on Jubilee USA, and the Grand Ole Opry in Nashville, Tennessee, becoming one of the youngest performers to ever appear. Billboard named her Most Promising Female Vocalist that year. Colonel Tom Parker, Elvis' manager, offered to take over her management, seeing the potential of a successful double "boy-girl" bill. But, safeguarding the young Janis Martin, her parents decided to not accept Parker's offer. RCA chose Martin to tour as a member of

the Jim Reeves show, and she continued recording rockabilly and country material that ended up
being successful on both charts, including "My
Boy Elvis", "Let's Elope Baby", her cover of Roy
Orbison's song "Ooby Dooby", and "Love Me to
Pieces". In the 1990's, Janis recorded with many
others, including Rosie Flores, and made many
appearances on revival shows, both in the USA and
Europe.

Jack Earls

In 1954, he formed a new band featuring guitarist Johnny Black (Bill Black's brother). This band
recorded a demo at Sam Phillips's recording studio
in mid-1955, "A Fool for Lovin' You" (written by
Earls himself). Phillips expressed interest, but told
him he'd need to find a new backing band. Earls
had Black move to upright bass. Their next recording session for Phillips resulted in the songs "Slow
Down" and "Hey Jim". Phillips released "Slow
Down" on his own Sun Records under the name
Jack Earls & the Jimbos, and the song became a
regional hit, although Earls was unable to tour
behind the record due to family obligations. Earls
recorded several further songs for Sun, but none of
them were released until many years later.

Earls' contract with Sun expired in what he says
to be around September 1966, and, despite being
contacted by Meteor and King, Earls declined to
record; although he did occasionally perform in
Memphis until he and his family moved to Detroit
in 1963. In the 1990s, Earls noted the growing
interest in rockabilly in Europe, and travelled to
England, where he became a star on the country

revival circuit. Subsequently, his output was re-released on Bear Family Records, and he toured Europe and America into the 2000s.

Ronnie Dawson

Ronnie Dawson was a rockabilly singer, guitarist and drummer, nicknamed 'The Blond Bomber'. Although he achieved regional success in the 1950s, his popularity peaked internationally with tours in the 1980s and 1990s. He formed his first band, Ronnie Dee & the D-Men, in 1956, and appeared regularly on the Big D Jamboree radio show in Dallas. The group's first record, a version of Jack Rhodes' song, "Action Packed", was issued in late 1958 on the Back Beat label. His second record, "Rockin' Bones", credited to "The Blond Bomber" Ronnie Dawson, was released in 1959, and again failed to chart. He performed with the well-established western swing group the Light Crust Doughboys for a time between 1957 and 1960.

In the 1980s, a resurgence of interest in rockabilly music, especially in England, prompted Dawson to tour Britain for the first time in 1986. Dawson continued to perform after developing throat cancer. His last live appearance was in early 2003 at the Rockabilly Rave in England, after which he returned to America and passed away in Dallas on September 30, 2003, at the age of 64.

Glen Glenn

He was born Orin Glenn Troutman in Joplin, Missouri, and in 1948 relocated with his parents to San Dimas, California. In the early 1950s, he formed a duo called the Missouri Mountain Boys with guitarist Gary Lambert, and began playing country music in bars in Los Angeles. They soon began performing on local television shows, and met singer and guitarist Eddie Cochran, who became a formative influence. Troutman began using the stage name Glen Trout, and began touring and recording demo records, often without Lambert. In late 1957, he signed with Era Records in Los Angeles, adopted the name Glen Glenn, and in January 1958 his first single was released, "Everybody's Movin", backed with "I'm Glad My Baby's Gone".

He was soon drafted, and, while Era continued to release his records, he was unable to promote them. After leaving the Army in 1960, he transferred to the Dore label and made some more pop-oriented recordings, which were unsuccessful. He continued to perform occasionally with Lambert, while also working outside the music industry. In 1977, Ace Records in Britain released a compilation of his rockabilly recordings, and his career was reinvigorated. He recorded a new album with Lambert in 1984, and continued to perform in clubs in California, as well as making occasional tours in Britain and Europe. He died on March 18, 2022, at the age of 87.

Warren Smith

Smith took up the guitar to while away his evenings while in the United States Air Force stationed in San Antonio, Texas. By the time of his discharge from the service, he had decided to make a career of music. He moved to West Memphis, Arkansas, and successfully auditioned to play the Cotton Club, a local nightclub. The steel guitarist Stan Kesler, who was playing there with the Snearly Ranch Boys, immediately spotted Smith's potential and took him to Sun Records to audition for Sam Phillips, with the Snearly Ranch Boys providing backup.

Phillips liked what he heard and decided that "Rock 'n' Roll Ruby", a song credited to Johnny Cash, would be Smith's first record. (Smith later claimed that the song was actually written by George Jones and sold to Cash for $40.). Smith recorded it on February 5, 1956. Phillips, playing it safe in case rock 'n' roll did not maintain its popularity, released it with a country crooner, aptly named "I'd Rather Be Safe Than Sorry", on the flip side. By May 26, "Rock 'n' Roll Ruby" had reached number 1 on the local pop chart; this record, his first for Sun, went on to outsell the first Sun releases by Elvis Presley, Johnny Cash and Carl Perkins.

In August 1956, Smith went back to the Sun Records studio to record his second release, "Ubangi Stomp", an infectious rocker with crude lyrics and vocals suggesting an African chief with the syntax of a movie Indian. For the B-side, he recorded the classic ballad "Black Jack David", a song that originated in early 18th-century Britain and survived in various forms in the mountains of the American South; it may be the oldest song ever recorded by a rock 'n' roll performer. Although a resounding artistic success, this record did not sell as well as Smith's debut.

In 1957, Smith recorded "So Long, I'm Gone", a song written by Roy Orbison. It became his biggest hit for Sun, peaking at number 74 on the Billboard national chart. But Sun had no cash to promote it, as Sam Phillips had put every dollar Sun had behind Jerry Lee Lewis's "Whole Lotta Shakin' Goin On". Smith continued to make rockabilly records for Sun, including a cover version of Slim Harpo's "Got Love If You Want It" (recorded in October 1957), but these records did not do well commercially. Toward the end of 1958, seeing his future in country music, he cut a final record for Sun, a cover version of Don Gibson's "Sweet Sweet Girl". In spite of a review in Billboard calling it "ultra commercial", this record also did not sell well. Like other artists such as Sonny Burgess, Hayden Thompson, Billy Lee Riley and Ray Harris, Smith had little success on the charts. He then decided to leave Sun Records.

In 1959, Smith and his wife and son moved from Mississippi to California, settling in Sherman Oaks, not far from Johnny and Vivian Cash. Cash offered Smith a spot on his show, but Smith turned it down, seeing himself as a headliner, not a supporting player.

In early 1960, Smith signed a contract with Liberty Records and immediately had a hit with "I Don't Believe I'll Fall in Love Today", which went to number 5 on the Billboard country and Western chart. This record and subsequent releases were mostly country songs for Liberty, with some success, and Smith toured with his band from 1960 to 1965.

On August 17, 1965, Smith suffered severe back injuries in a car crash in LaGrange, Texas. It took nearly a year for him to recover. By this time, his contract with Liberty had lapsed. He made several attempts to restart his career, first with a small, virtually amateur label called Skill Records, and then with Mercury Records, but addictions to pills and alcohol held him back. Eventually, he was convicted of robbing a pharmacy and sentenced to an 18-month term in an Alabama prison.

After his release from prison, Smith again tried to restart his career. He got some publicity from the rockabilly revival in the late 1970s. In 1977 he was invited to appear at London's Rainbow Theatre, on a bill featuring Charlie Feathers, Buddy Knox and Jack Scott. To his shock, Smith was received in London with standing ovations. His reception in England boosted his spirits and, upon his return to the United States, he began to perform with new-found vigour. In November 1978, Smith and fellow Sun alumnus Ray Smith toured Europe, again with great success. Smith died of a heart attack in 1980, at 47 years of age, while preparing for another European tour.

Mac Curtis

Curtis began playing guitar at the age of 12, entering local talent competitions. In 1954, he formed a band with two classmates, Jim and Ken Galbraith. They played at school events, but during one of the events their show was shut down due to sexually suggestive on-stage movements. The group played locally, and in 1955 was offered a deal with King Records, who released their debut single, "If

I Had Me a Woman". Soon afterwards, Alan Freed heard the group and invited them to play on his Christmas radio special in 1956.

Curtis returned to finish school in 1957, and then became a disc jockey in Seoul, Korea, after joining the military. Upon his return in 1960, he continued working as a DJ in the South, and released a few albums. As rockabilly grew in popularity in the 1970s, he began recording with Ray Campi, and signed to Ronnie Weiser's Rollin' Rock Records. As a singer he was still active in the 1980s and 1990s. He was later elected to the Rockabilly Hall of Fame. He died on September 16, 2013, aged 74, following injuries received in a car accident a month earlier, after which he had undergone rehabilitation at a nursing home.

Jack Scott

Born Giovanni Domenico Scafone Jr., and described as "undeniably the greatest Canadian rock and roll singer of all time", he grew up listening to hillbilly music, and was taught to play the guitar by his mother, Laura. As a teenager, he pursued a singing career and recorded as "Jack Scott". At the age of 18, he formed the Southern Drifters.

After leading the band for three years, he signed to ABC-Paramount Records as a solo artist in 1957. Having recorded two good-selling local hits for ABC-Paramount in 1957, he switched to the Carlton record label and had a double-sided national hit in 1958 with "Leroy" / "My True Love". The record sold over one million copies, earning Scott his first gold disc. Later in 1958, "With Your

Love" reached the Top 40. In all, 6 of 12 songs on his first album became hit singles. On most of these tracks he was backed up by the vocal group, The Chantones.

He served in the United States Army during most of 1959, just after "Goodbye Baby" made the Top Ten. 1959 also saw him chart with "The Way I Walk". Most of his Carlton master tapes were believed lost or destroyed, until Rollercoaster Records in England released a vinyl EP, "Jack Scott Rocks", and CD, The Way I Walk, which were for the most part mastered from original tapes, rather than the disc dubs used for previous reissues. Scott died of congestive heart failure on December 12, 2019, in Warren, Michigan, aged 83.

The Jodimars

They were an American rock 'n' roll band formed in the summer of 1955, and remained active until 1958. The band was created by former members of Bill Haley & His Comets, who had quit that group in a salary dispute. In fact, the day they quit, it was announced that "Rock Around the Clock" had reached Number One. The name of the group was derived from the first letters of the first names of the founding members: Joey Ambrose (real name Joey d'Ambrosio) (saxophone), Dick Boccelli (under the name "Dick Richards") (vocals and drums), and Marshall Lytle (string bass). Other members included Chuck Hess (guitar), Jim Buffington (drums), Bob Simpson (Piano), and Max Daffner (drums). During the summer of 1955, Lytle, Ambrose and Richards, who were paid on a set salary (as opposed to the other two Comets, pianist Johnny Grande and steel guitar player Billy Williamson, who were considered partners with Haley), requested a pay raise. Their request was denied by either Haley's management, or by Haley himself (accounts vary). During that summer, unknown to Haley, the trio recruited a couple of other musicians and recorded a few demo tapes - including a version of a Haley composition, "Rock-a-Beatin' Boogie". This won the group a recording contract with Capitol Records, and the group subsequently resigned from the Comets. The group's first recordings on Capitol came out in late 1955, and the band scored a few minor hits such as "Well Now, Dig This" and "Let's All Rock Together". In 1956, the Jodimars became one of the first rock 'n' roll acts to take up residence in Las Vegas showrooms. Soon after, they left Capitol and recorded for smaller labels with no success. By 1958, the band had virtually broken up.

The Collins Kids

They were an American rockabilly duo featuring Lawrencine "Lorrie" Collins and her younger brother Lawrence "Larry" Collins.Their hits in the 1950s as youngsters, such as "Hop, Skip and Jump", "Beetle Bug Bop" and "Hoy Hoy", were infectious singing, and their playing crossed over generations. Larry, a lightning-fingered guitar whiz at age 10, was known for playing a double-neck Mosrite guitar like his mentor, Joe Maphis. Lorrie dated Ricky Nelson, and Larry appeared in the film "Every Which Way But Loose".

The Collins siblings continued to perform together in the mid-1960s, appearing as regulars on the

Canadian music program Star Route, and making a guest appearance on the September 8, 1965, edition of Shindig! The duo reunited for a rockabilly revival concert in England in 1993, and performed regularly together until Lorrie's death in 2018 in Reno, Nevada, from complications of a fall, aged 76.

Selected Rock 'n' roll Performers

Elvis Presley

"The King of rock 'n' roll", a soubriquet that has been questioned many times over the years, especially as it was media generated, and whose probable source was Colonel Tom Parker, in an effort to keep Elvis' name in the public eye during his Army service. Without doubt, Elvis was the key that unlocked the rock 'n' roll door, allowing others to come pouring through.

He began at SUN records, performing what is now called rockabilly, though within 18 months he had left for RCA and began setting the standard by which others were compared. Also, without doubt, the year of 1956 was his best, as were the first two films, "Loving You" and "King Creole". After fulfilling his military service obligations, he emerged as never quite the same. Tom Parker signed him up to a series of soppy films that followed an increasingly tired looking format, and became worse and worse, although there were some exceptions, such as "Charro".

Once Elvis had exerted some authority, he went back to touring, the highlight of which was the 68-comeback special, where he was back to his best and clearly enjoying the experience. After that he then began a long-term residency in Las Vegas, where his stage show was developed into a more and more elaborate spectacle.

It was around this time that he began to put on weight and suffer medical problems, alleviating the symptoms with a bewildering cocktail of prescribed and non-prescribed drugs. His physical appearance got worse as he put on weight, and became almost a parody of himself. He passed away on August 16, 1977, aged 42. Even this didn't deter the Colonel; his autopsy was made public, and RCA began to re-release almost everything and anything, including previously unreleased recordings, and even some acquired bootlegs. Elvis Presly's estate has made more money since his death than he ever did whilst alive.

Chuck Berry

Chuck Berry is something of an enigma. Is he to be classed into R&B, rockabilly or rock 'n' roll? He originally auditioned for Leonard Chess with a blues number, "In the Wee Wee Hours", but his first big hit was "Maybellene", an adaption of a country song, called "Ida red". Apparently, Chuck once commented that the only "Maybellene" he ever knew was a cow!

Nicknamed the "Father of Rock and Roll", he refined and developed rhythm and blues into the major elements that made rock and roll distinctive, with songs such as "Maybellene", "Roll Over Beethoven", "Rock and Roll Music" and "Johnny B. Goode". He wrote lyrics that focused on teen life and consumerism, and developed a music style that included guitar solos and showmanship.

The problem with Chuck Berry was that he was an intelligent black man, and thus, to the authorities, dangerous. With the racial problems and tension in America at the time, he was always going to be a target. He was sentenced to three years in prison in January 1962 for violating the Mann Act, which stated that it was illegal to transport a minor over a state line for sexual purposes. Upon his release he continued to write and record good rock 'n' roll songs, but by that time the rock 'n' roll heyday had gone.

Following a four-month spell in jail for tax evasion, he continued his career, always insisting on being paid in cash, but by then was mainly playing nostalgia-based events and festivals.

In 1972, Chess released the critically acclaimed album, 'The London Chuck Berry Sessions'. Side one of the album consists of studio recordings, engineered by Geoff Calver; side two features three live performances recorded by the Pye Mobile Unit at the Lanchester Arts Festival in Coventry, England. At the end of the live section, the recording includes the sounds of festival management trying in vain to get the audience to leave so that the next performers, Pink Floyd, can take the stage; the crowd begins chanting "We want Chuck!". The album propelled Chuck Berry back into the spotlight, resulting in a return to the charts with a novelty song, My Ding a Ling, that was at best risqué, and arguably one of the worst recordings he ever made. Berry was among the first musicians to be inducted into the Rock and Roll Hall of Fame on its opening in 1986; he was cited for having "laid the groundwork for not only a rock and roll sound, but a rock and roll stance." Chuck Berry was found dead, possibly from a heart attack, on March 18, 2017, aged 90.

Jerry Lee Lewis

Known as "The Killer", Jerry Lee Lewis was the wildest of the original rock 'n' rollers, both on and off stage. Lewis made his first recordings in 1952 at Cosimo Matassa's J&M Studio in New Orleans, Louisiana, but his first significant recordings in 1956 at Sun Records in Memphis, Tennessee. He had arrived at SUN mainly thanks to the fact that Sam Phillips had sold Elvis' contract to RCA, which allowed him to introduce new artists. Billy Lee Riley, had been under the impression that Sam Phillips would be backing and promoting him, so was disappointed when Jerry Lee was the main focus of attention, a fact that Billy Lee bemoaned most of his life. But, when one looks at the Jerry Lee Lewis output, it isn't perhaps hard to see why. "Crazy Arms" sold 300,000 copies in the Southern United States, but it was his 1957 hit "Whole Lotta Shakin' Goin' On" that shot Lewis to worldwide fame. He followed this with the major hits "Great Balls of Fire", "Breathless", and "High School Confidential".

As a teenager, Lewis studied at the Southwest Bible Institute in Waxahachie, Texas, before being thrown out for playing a 'worldly' boogie-woogie version of "My God Is Real", and that early incident foreshadowed his lifelong conflict over his faith in God and his love of playing "the Devil's music". Lewis had a recorded argument with Sam Phillips during the recording session for "Great Balls of Fire", a song he initially refused to record because he considered it blasphemous ("How can... How can the Devil save souls? What are you talkin' about?" he asks Phillips during one heated exchange.)

It was whilst on tour in England in 1957, that Jerry Lee's career fell apart. It was discovered that he was married to the 15-year-old Myra Gale Brown, who was also his first cousin once removed. The tour ended after just 4 dates, and Jerry Lee returned to the United States with his reputation in tatters. His popularity quickly eroded following the scandal and, with few exceptions such as a cover of Ray Charles's "What'd I Say", he did not have much chart success in the early 1960s, although his live performances at this time were increasingly wild and energetic. His 1964 live album Live at the Star Club, Hamburg is regarded by many music journalists and fans in general as one of the wildest and greatest live rock albums ever.

In 1968, Lewis made a transition into country music, and had hits with songs such as "Another Place, Another Time". This reignited his career, and throughout the late 1960s and 1970s he regularly topped the country-western charts; throughout his seven-decade career, Lewis had 30 songs reach the Top 10 on the Billboard Country and Western Chart. His No. 1 country hits included "To Make Love Sweeter for You", "There Must Be More to Love Than This", "Would You Take Another Chance on Me", and "Me and Bobby McGee".

Lewis's successes continued throughout the decades and he embraced his rock 'n' roll past with songs such as a cover of The Big Bopper's

"Chantilly Lace", and Mack Vickery's "Rockin' My Life Away". In the 21st Century, Lewis continued to tour around the world and released new albums. His 2006 album Last Man Standing was his bestselling release, with over a million copies worldwide. This was followed by Mean Old Man in 2010, another of his bestselling album.

Lewis was married seven times, including bigamous marriages and the marriage with his underage cousin. He had six children during his marriages.

Lewis had been known as the last man standing, after his hit album, but he was also the last of the big-name rock 'n' rollers left still alive. Lewis had a minor stroke in Memphis on February 28, 2019, and had to cancel several appearances. Lewis died at his home on October 28, 2022, in Nesbit, Mississippi, at the age of 87, although his death was mistakenly reported by TMZ two days before he died, with a representative stating that TMZ had reported "erroneously off of an anonymous tip". Lewis' funeral was held on November 5, 2022, in his hometown of Ferriday, Louisiana. The service was officiated by his cousin Jimmy Swaggart and Swaggart's son.

Eddie Cochran

Cochran was involved with music from an early age, playing in the school band and teaching himself to play blues guitar. In 1954, he formed a duet with the guitarist Hank Cochran (no relation). Together they performed some of rockabilly's best-known tunes, and Eddie established himself as a guitarist of real talent. When they split the following year, Eddie began a songwriting career with Jerry Capehart. His first success came when he performed the song "Twenty Flight Rock" in the film The Girl Can't Help It, starring Jayne Mansfield. Soon afterwards he signed a recording contract with Liberty Records and his first record for the label, "Sittin' in the Balcony", rose to number 18 on the Billboard charts. He went on to record some of rock 'n' roll's most beloved songs, such as "Twenty Flight Rock", "Summertime Blues", "C'mon Everybody" and "Somethin' Else", he captured teenage frustration and desire in the mid-1950s and early 1960s.Much Like Buddy Holly and Norman Petty in Clovis, New Mexico, he experimented with multitrack recording, distortion techniques and overdubbing, even on his earliest singles. He played the guitar, piano, bass, and drums. Towards the end of his career he began experimenting with production, and became a mentor for some up-and-coming performers, including Skeets McDonald, Troyce Key and Wynn Stewart. He also guested on other performers' records, such as Johnny Burnette and Gene Vincent.

Cochran was on tour in the United Kingdom from January through April 1960. He and his friend and fellow performing artist, Gene Vincent had just finished performing at the last of their scheduled concerts at the Bristol Hippodrome on April 16, a Saturday night. They were travelling along the Bath Road in a taxi (a cream-coloured 1960 model Ford Consul Mark II saloon) from Bristol towards

London. In addition to Cochran and Vincent, the other passengers in the vehicle were Sharon Sheeley, (a 20-year-old songwriter, who was also Cochran's fiancée at the time), Patrick Tompkins (the tour manager, 29 years old), and George Martin (the 19-year-old taxi driver). At about 11:50 p.m. that night, Martin lost control of the vehicle, which crashed into a concrete lamppost at Rowden Hill in Chippenham. At the moment of impact, Cochran (who was seated in the centre of the back seat) threw himself over Sheeley to shield her. The force of the collision caused the left rear passenger door to open, and Cochran was ejected from the vehicle, sustaining a massive traumatic brain injury from blunt force trauma to the skull. The vehicle was later determined to be travelling at an excessive speed, with no other vehicle involved in the incident. Cochran never regained consciousness and died at 4:10 p.m. the following day – Easter Sunday. Cochran's body was flown home and, after a funeral service, was buried on April 25 at Forest Lawn Memorial Park in Cypress, California.

Gene Vincent

Born Eugene Vincent Craddock, he dropped out of school in 1952 at the age of 17, and enlisted in the United States Navy. As he was under the age of enlistment, his parents signed the forms allowing him to enter. Vincent completed boot camp and joined the fleet as a crewman aboard the fleet oiler USS Chukawan, with a two-week training period in the repair ship USS Amphion, before returning to the Chukawan. He never saw combat, but completed a Korean War deployment. He sailed home from Korean waters aboard the battleship USS Wisconsin, but was not part of the ship's company. He'd always planned a career in the Navy, thus re-enlisted and, and with his re-enlistment pay, purchased a Triumph motorcycle. Shortly afterwards he was involved in an accident, when a truck hit him, and his leg was shattered. Vincent left the Navy shortly afterwards, having refused to have it amputated, but had a distinct limp, and was forced to wear a steel sheath for the rest of his life.

Vincent then became involved in the Norfolk music scene, forming his own band, the Blue Caps. The name came from the nickname for enlisted servicemen in the Navy. Pretty soon they were playing in Norfolk and the surrounding area, where they won a talent contest organized by a local radio DJ, "Sheriff Tex" Davis, who then became Vincent's manager.

"Sheriff Tex" Davis arranged for a recording session for a new song that Vincent had written, called "Be-Bop-a-Lula"; he then took it to Capitol Records who, like most other labels, were looking for new young talent to combat RCA's signing of Elvis. They signed Vincent on and released "Be-Bop-a-Lula" as a B side to "Woman Love". In a very short time, "Be-Bop-a-Lula", which was the B Side, remember, was already gaining attention from the public and radio DJs.

The song was picked up and played by other U.S. radio stations (obscuring the original A-side song) and became a big hit, peaking at number 7 and spending 20 weeks on the Billboard pop chart, as well as reaching number 5 and spending 17 weeks on the Cash Box chart, thus launching Vincent's career as a rock 'n' roll star.

After "Be-Bop-a-Lula" became a hit, Vincent and His Blue Caps were unable to follow it up with the same level of commercial success, although they released critically acclaimed songs like "Race with the Devil", "Who Slapped John" and "Bluejean Bop", another million-selling disc. Vincent and his band were known for their hard-working no-nonsense style, although the original line up was disrupted when Cliff Gallup left to be replaced by Russell Williford as the new guitarist. Williford played and toured Canada with Vincent in late 1956, but left the group in early 1957. Gallup came back to do the next album and then left again. Williford came back and exited again, before Johnny Meeks joined the band.

The group had another hit in 1957 with "Lotta Lovin'". Vincent was awarded gold records for two million sales of "Be-Bop-a-Lula", and 1.5 million sales of "Lotta Lovin'". The same year he toured the east coast of Australia with Little Richard and Eddie Cochran, drawing audiences totalling 72,000 to their Sydney Stadium concerts. Vincent also made an appearance in the film The Girl Can't Help It, with Jayne Mansfield, performing "Be-Bop-a-Lula" with the Blue Caps in a rehearsal room. "Dance to the Bop" was released by Capitol Records on October 28, 1957. On November 17, 1957, Vincent and His Blue Caps performed the song on the nationally broadcast television program The Ed Sullivan Show. The song spent nine weeks on the Billboard chart, and peaked at number 23 on January 23, 1958. It was Vincent's last American hit single. The song was used in the movie Hot Rod Gang for a dance rehearsal scene featuring dancers doing the West Coast Swing.

As the initial impact of rock 'n' roll was waning, and the fact that Vincent had problems with both the US Tax authorities and the Musicians Union, he left for Great Britain, and appeared on Jack Good's "Boy meets Girl" TV series. Good is credited with the transformation of Vincent's image, and had him dress in black leather and asked him to exaggerate his limp. It made such an impact that, years later, Ian Dury, a Gene Vincent fan and victim of polio, would adopt similar mannerisms when performing on stage. Gene Vincent was always more popular in Europe, especially in England and France, and was still performing until he died at the age of 36 on October 12, 1971, from a combination of a ruptured ulcer, internal haemorrhage and heart failure. Vincent's musical legacy is enormous, and he remains one of the big favourites amongst rock 'n' roll and rockabilly crowds.

Buddy Holly
One of the most important figures from the 1950's, whose legacy continues to this day, Buddy was actually Charles Hardin Holley, but a misspelling of his surname gave the world 'Holly'. The name Buddy came from the American tradition of using that nickname for the youngest child in a family. Buddy originally got together with Bob Montgomery as the 'Buddy and Bob' show,

playing local dances and radio station events. Buddy claimed his musical direction changed when he saw Elvis Presley, who toured through Lubbock, his home town.

Buddy formed the Crickets, consisting of Jerry Allison on drums, Niki Sullivan on rhythm guitar, and Joe B. Mauldin on bass. They first turned up on vinyl after they recorded for Decca in Nashville. That first session threw up, "Blue Days, Black Nights", one of the most underrated rockabilly tunes of all time, and several other tunes. However, Decca declined to keep Buddy on contract, and he met up with Norman Petty in Clovis, New Mexico, and a lifelong bond was formed. Together they would go on to create some of the most memorable rock 'n' roll ever recorded, utilising pioneering studio techniques that are now taken for granted, but at the time were innovative and new. Strangely, and somewhat ironically, Buddy and the Crickets were signed to the Corel label, which was actually a division of Decca records!

Reading down a list of the hit songs that Buddy wrote and recorded is almost like carving a whole slice of 1950's rockabilly and rock 'n' roll. "That'll be the Day", "Peggy Sue", "Rock Around with Ollie Vee", "Maybe Baby", "Midnight Shift", and many more.

Buddy split with the Crickets and Norman Petty after he met and married Maria Elanor Santiago, and moved to New York. There was also a dispute over royalties that were or were not paid. Buddy began experimenting with some new tunes he had written and, whilst still signed for Corel, saw some of them released as singles. It was in early 1958 that Buddy joined The Winter Dance Party, a tour which began in Milwaukee, Wisconsin, on January 23, 1959. The tour was badly organised; the amount of travel involved created logistical problems, as the distance between venues had not been considered when scheduling performances. Adding to the problem, the unheated tour buses twice broke down in freezing weather, with dire consequences. It was one of the harshest winters ever in the Midwest and Holly's drummer Carl Bunch was hospitalized for frostbite to his toes (sustained while aboard the bus), so Holly decided to seek other transportation. On February 2, before their appearance in Clear Lake, Iowa, Holly chartered a four-seat Beechcraft Bonanza airplane from the Dwyer Flying Service in Mason City, Iowa, for Jennings, Allsup and himself. Holly's idea was to depart following the show at the Surf Ballroom in Clear Lake and fly to their next venue in Moorhead, Minnesota, via Fargo, North Dakota, allowing them time to rest and launder their clothes and avoid a rigorous bus journey. Immediately after the Clear Lake show (which ended just before midnight), Allsup agreed to flip a coin for the seat with the young star, Ritchie Valens. Valens called heads; when he won, he reportedly said, "That's the first time I've ever won anything in my life." Allsup later opened a restaurant/bar in Fort Worth, Texas, called Heads Up Saloon. Waylon Jennings also tossed a coin for the last seat with J. P. Richardson (the Big Bopper), who had influenza and complained that the tour bus was too cold and uncomfortable for a man of his size. After he lost the toss, Waylon jokingly remarked that he hoped the plane crashed. That flippant remark haunted him for the rest of his life. The pilot, Roger Peterson, took off in inclement weather, even though he was not certified to fly by instruments only. Shortly after 12:55 am on February 3, 1959, Holly, Valens, Richardson and Peterson were killed when the aircraft crashed into a cornfield five miles northwest of Mason City shortly after take-off.

Holly was 22 years old. The news dominated the airwaves and newspapers for weeks afterwards, and Corel released a song, "It Doesn't Matter Any More", which became an instant multimillion selling worldwide hit. Since his death, Holly's contribution to music has been recognised on numerous occasions, with many others covering the tunes that he wrote and recorded, and at least two films have been made about him. It is poignant to suggest that without Buddy Holly, his innovative studio techniques, and his music, the direction music took in subsequent years might not have happened without his contribution.

Selected Current Rockabilly and Rock 'n' roll Performers

The Stray Cats

The group, whose style was based upon the sounds of Sun Records artists and other artists from the 1950s, was heavily influenced by Eddie Cochran, Carl Perkins, Gene Vincent, and Bill Haley & His Comets.The Stray Cats originally began in New York, named as the Tom Cats, but whilst they achieved interest, there wasn't enough to sustain their momentum, although they had developed a cult following in the New York music scene. Brian Setzer, the band's leader, heard that there was a revival of interest in rockabilly and rock 'n' roll in London, so the band travelled to England in 1979 and, according to spin at the time, slept rough as they had nowhere to stay and no gigs planned. However, they managed to get a couple of small gigs, but noticed that clubs and pubs would not book the same band on consecutive nights, there-fore used various names, always with the 'Cats' as the second part of the name.

In 1980, they met Dave Edmonds, who was well known as a musician and producer, specialising in retro and vintage music. He offered to work with the band and, with a number of record companies showing interest, Edmonds took them into a studio to record their first album, "Stray Cats", which was released by Arista records in 1981. In that year the band also hit the British charts with three records, "Runaway Boys", "Stray Cat Strut" and "Rock This Town". In America, EMI was interested and made a compilation album, "Built for Speed"; tracks were culled from the first two UK albums, and went on to sell over a million copies.

Musical and personal conflicts began to emerge in the ways the individual members handled their new-found success; Phantom married actress Britt Ekland, while Setzer made guest appearances with stars like Bob Dylan and Stevie Nicks, and became the concert guitarist for Robert Plant's Honeydrippers side project. In late 1984, the band added former BMT's guitarist and Long Island native Tommy Byrnes on second guitar and harmony vocals, and after a European and US tour which ended at the 1984 Louisiana World Exposition, parted ways. The decision to end the band was Setzer's, but it left the other members aggrieved. In an interview, Setzer pleaded restlessness as his motivation: "It's just that I didn't get that great feeling anymore... I had five good years of that, but then I got bored with it. In the last year I stopped getting that feeling, that great kick that twisted in my gut." Reflecting in 2012, Setzer said "it was silly to break up the Stray Cats at the peak of our success."

Individual band members went on to solo projects with varying degrees of success, but have returned as The Stray Cats occasionally, notably for their 25th anniversary. Brian Setzer has been acclaimed for his guitar techniques, and has even authored books and videos on his techniques.

Darrel Higham

Arguably the UK's top rockabilly/rock 'n' roll guitarist, Higham began his career playing in various bands, until he met bass player Mick Wigfall, and in the mid 1990's formed Darrel Higham and the Enforcers. Higham is a huge Eddie Cochran fan, and therefore it was an honour for him to be asked to perform with The Kelly Four - Eddie Cochran's last touring band - for a six-month period in 1992 for gigs and recordings in the US.

In 1996, Higham played the parts of Eddie Cochran and Scotty Moore in Jack Good's "Elvis the Musical", which played at The Prince of Wales Theatre in London. The role led him to be invited to tour as Eddie Cochran, playing in tribute events for a couple of years.

In 2002, Higham married Irish singer Imelda May (nee` Clabby), and appeared as lead guitarist in her band as she proceeded to take the British music scene by storm. They divorced in 2015, and Darrel left her band to re-form and concentrate on touring and gigging with The Enforcers.Higham has performed with a host of musicians world-wide, including Brian Setzer, Rocky Burnette (son of Johnny), Jeff Beck and many more. Higham remains in demand, is recognised as having a unique talent, and continues to tour and gig to this day.

Eva Eastwood

Eva Östlund, better known by her stage name Eva Eastwood (born in Örebro, Sweden, on 25 September 1967), is a Swedish songwriter and singer who sings rockabilly and rock 'n' roll songs. In 1997, early in her career, she travelled to Nashville to do some recording. She was offered a lucrative contract, but she chose to go back home as she was contracted to record an album in Sweden. Soon after she formed the band, The Major Keys, and made releases crediting Eva Eastwood and the Major Keys on the small Tail Records label based in Jönköping.

Eastwood was invited to appear with the band at the Hemsby Rock & Roll Weekender in England, and was an immediate hit. She is blessed with 'perfect pitch'... an ability to hit the correct notes immediately, without much rehearsal. Eastwood also writes songs and, despite the sometimes quaint English she uses, her rockabilly and rock 'n' roll output are universally praised.

In 2005, she took part in Allsång på Skansen, a sing-along TV show from Skansen, performing "Vårt liv i repris" from her album En ny stil i stan which proved to be a turning point in her career. Eastwood won the Millencolin Music Prize 2010, becoming the first woman to do so. In 2011, she returned to the same stage singing the title track "Lyckost" from her similarly named album. Whilst appearances at rock 'n' roll and rockabilly events are few and far between, once announced, there is generally an enthusiasm and eagerness to see her perform live.

Jack Rabbit Slim

The inspiration for the band was Bob Butefoy, who had originally formed Bob and the Bearcats with Darrel Higham, Nick Hoadley and Les Curtis. Jack Rabbit Slim, who took their name from the film "Pulp Fiction", emerged onto the scene with a bang around 2006. With Bob's energetic frontman antics driving the band along, and backed by Tom Hayes' on lead guitar and Nick Linton Smith on bass, JRS quickly became THE band to see on the rockabilly scene, recording with Alan Wilson's Western Star label. So popular were the band, that they were quickly invited to tour in the USA; however, some members of the band decided to leave as they preferred not to travel, so Bob recruited new members and they hit the USA. The tour was a great success, although marred somewhat by threats from the Jack Daniels Brewery who objected to the similarity of the band's logo to their own label.

Jack Rabbit Slim released over ten albums on Western Star before calling it a day around 2020, although in 2023 reformed and released a new album, 'Hard to forget'.

Jack Baymoore & the Bandits

Anyone listening to Jack Baymoore on stage might be forgiven for thinking that Baymoore came from the heart of Texas; however, in reality, Baymoore, real name Kent Vikmo, hails from Sweden. On stage, the band are precise, as tight as anyone would want from any band. Baymoore has also made a number of tribute projects. Very notably he was in the Johnny Cash tribute band, the Tennessee Drifters.

He also played critically acclaimed tribute gigs, singing Elvis Presley songs, and has appeared in a number of rockabilly compilations. Due to their location and commitments of band members, UK appearances are few and far between, but when they happen, they play to packed out venues and enjoy enthusiastic audiences.

Big Sandy & the Fly Right Boys

An American rockabilly and Western swing band from California, comprised of Big Sandy, aka Robert Williams, renowned lead guitarist, Ashley Kingman, Ricky McCann and Kevin Stewart. The band are known for their versatility, which encompasses rockabilly, Western swing, folk, bluegrass, Cajun, mariachi, rock and roll, swing and country. Originally formed in 1988, they have become one of the world's most beloved Roots acts, drawing from the deep musical waters that flow just beneath the surface of Rock & Roll's fertile soil.

After nearly 35 years on the road, and more than two dozen releases to their credit, they remain key figures on the ever-changing Americana circuit, both on record and in live appearances. The band has also been inducted into the Rockabilly Hall of Fame.

The Go Getters

In January of 1988, amidst the frozen badlands of Västerås, Sweden, a gang of vikings decided to heat things up by forming a rockabilly trio. They would call themselves the Go Getters. Thirty-five years later the band is still going strong. Led by stand-up drummer and chief songwriter Peter Sandberg on lead vocals, the Go Getters have electrified audiences around the world with their own custom blend of arse-kickin' rockabilly boogie.

After appearing on several compilation albums in the late 1980's, the Go Getters released their first single, "You Don't Love Me", in 1992. The song soon topped the European roots music charts, and led to the release of their debut LP, "Real Gone!". The success of these records fuelled a demand for the group throughout Europe, where they toured without mercy for the better part of a decade. In addition to their own shows, the Go Getters have backed many of the 50's biggest rockabilly stars, including Sleepy La Beef, Ray Sharp, Larry Donn, Johnny Powers and the late, great, Ronnie Dawson.

The group embarked on their first tour of the United States in 1995, playing Chicago, Detroit and Minneapolis, before finally hitting Fairmont Indiana, where they rocked the Rebel Weekender to a frenzy, proving that a gang of Vikings could still conquer a continent. In May of 1996 they also made their long-awaited debut appearance at the Hemsby Rock & Roll Weekender 16 in the U.K., inciting their fans to near riot. In 1998 they played the Viva Las Vegas Rockabilly Weekender, where their performance was said to have raised the candlepower of the Vegas skyline to that of a nuclear blast!

Regular performers on all of the major rock 'n roll and rockabilly festivals, the Go Getters are considered THE band to see for many of the attendees.

CHAPTER NINE
Other recommended reading and viewing

Go Cat Go!	Craig Morrison	University of Illinois Press
Teddy Boy Wars	Michael Macwiwee	Milo Books Ltd
A Rocket in my Pocket	Max De`charge	Serpent's tale
Last Train to Memphis	Peter Gulralnick	Little, Brown & Company
Careless Love	" "	" "
Buddy Holly – his life and music	John L Goldrosen	Grenada publishing
Buddy – The Bography	Phillip Norman	MacMillen
The real rhythm and blues	Hugh Gregory	Blandford A Cassell
Big Beat Heat – Alan Freed & the early years of rock n roll	John A Jackson	Schirmer Books
Teddy Boys – A Concise history	Ray Ferris & Julian Lord	Milo Books
Race with the devil - Gene Vincent's Life i n the fast lane	Susan Vanhecke	St Martins Press
Let the good times Roll - The story of Louis Jordan and his music	John Chiltern	Quartet Books
Jerry Lee Lewis my own Story	Rick Briggs	Cannongate books

FILMS

American Graffiti	1973	Directed by George Lucas
Rock Around the Clock	1956	Directed by Fred F. Sears.
Untamed Youth	1957	Directed by Howard H Koch
Rebel without a cause	1955	Directed by Nicholas Ray
Blackboard Jungle	1955	Directed by Richard Brooks
The Lords of Flatbush	1974	Directed by Martin Davidson and Stephen F. Verona.
Cry-Baby	1990	Directed by John Waters.
The Girl Can't Help It	1956	Directed by Frank Tashlin
Don't knock the rock	1956	Directed by Fred F. Sears
Go, Johnny, G0!	1959	Directed by Paul Landres & Piero Vivareli
American Hot Wax	1978	Directed by Floyd Mutrux
Walk the Line	2005	Directed by James Mangold
I Saw the Light	2015	Directed by Marc Abraham

ACKNOWLEDGEMENTS

With any work such as this, research is of vital importance, as is being able to read between the lines. A lot of my research was utilising stories and history that had been passed down to me as I was growing up and enjoying rockabilly and rock n' Roll music.

I also re-read selected titles from the small library of books that I have acquired over the years, some of which are listed under further reading. And lastly, I spent (too many) hours trawling through historical references to segregation in the USA.

However, credit where credit is due, and I hereby acknowledge and thank every one of the performers, that inspired me, and a lot of others that didn't, but whose music I still enjoy. I would also like to thank Tom Ingram for correcting some of the manuscript that involved him and also to Chrissie White for proof reading and she was a good choice to proof read and edit, because although she enjoys a bit of rock n' roll, she hasn't grown up with it as I have, therefore was unfamiliar with it's history, so she looked at this project with a different, more objective attitude. I therefore thank her for inspiring me to continually re-read and edit the manuscript at least four times, to make sure that the work was more readable.

'Wildkat' Mike George

ABOUT THE AUTHOR
'Wildkat' Mike George

Upon leaving school, Mike was a rock 'n' roll club DJ, playing at local social and youth clubs. He first got into music, working at the Finsbury Park Rainbow before serving in the British Army for 8 years. Following this he began working for BFBS (British Forces Broadcasting Service), based in Germany, where his rock 'n' roll show was beamed worldwide. Around this time, he also tried his hand at stand-up comedy.

On returning to the UK, he worked for a variety of radio stations, such as RTM (London) and

Devonair as well as a brief stint for the BBC. Since 2012 he has been broadcasting for Rockabilly Radio, an internet-based station that broadcasts 24/7 worldwide.

Mike is also a musician and singer, playing Double Bass and singing in bands such as Flashback, The Lynchburg Lockout, Dixie Fried and his current band, The Shotrods.

Mike has had two books published, and is an artist, cartoonist and illustrator – as well as being a devoted follower of Millwall F.C. He states that if he ever wrote his autobiography, it would be called, "Life at the blunt end".

Previous books:
Golden Days - The History of Maidstone United F.C. – Yore publications

The Fletcher Diaries – Published on Amazon & Kindle Unlimited.

Got a book in you?

PUBLISHING
victorpublishing.co.uk

This book is published by Victor Publishing.

Victor Publishing specialises in getting new and independent writers' work published worldwide in both paperback and Kindle format.

If you have a manuscript for a book of any genre (fiction, non-fiction, autobiographical, biographical or even reference or photographic/illustrative) and would like more information on how you can get your work published and on sale to the general public, please visit us at:

www.victorpublishing.co.uk

Printed in Great Britain
by Amazon

33032096R00106